WHO'S PADDLING YOUR CANOE?

Barbara Mikus

To my freind, neighbour, & sister - Teresa.
  This looked interesting, I
hope you enjoy it.

          Love
          Bethsaida

WHO'S PADDLING YOUR CANOE?
A Message of Transformation and
Surrendering Control of Your Life

By Barbara Mikus

© 2005 Barbara Mikus
All rights reserved.

ISBN # 1-894928-61-X

Printed by Word Alive Press

WORD ALIVE PRESS

Table of Contents

Foreword v

Introduction vii

1. Salvation: Getting into the Canoe 1

2. Discipleship & Restoration: Leaving a Restful Spot 11

3. Forgiveness: Stopping Along the Shore 21

4. Trust: Going a Different Route 31

5. Perseverance: Learning to Paddle the Canoe 39

6. Relationship: Taking on Other Passengers 51

7. Patience: Wanting to Paddle Faster 61

8. Honour: Submitting to a New Captain.............69

9. Love: Staying in the Canoe When You Are Afraid 77

10. Joy: Throwing Everything Out of the Canoe 85

11. Hope: Stranded with No Wind.......................97

12. Ministry: Stepping Out of the Canoe onto the Water.. 107

Conclusion 115

Foreword

My wife, Cheryl, and I have known Barb for over two decades and have had the privilege of walking with her throughout her journey of faith. We have served her and her family as pastors and friends.

We attest to the validity of this story of hidden pain & inner shame to victory in Christ. *Who's Paddling your Canoe* presents to the reader the deep desire of Barb's heart to "know God and make Him known." This has caused her to search for truth to discover the healing and freedom that comes from an honest, perseverant pursuit of Christ. Barb is a helper of humankind, a good friend and a woman of God, and this book represents her strong desire and generous spirit to assist people in discovering for themselves the "way out" from lives of insecurity, abuse, brokenness, fear, depression and anxiety into the wholeness found in Christ.

The scriptures have played a vital role in her life and it is fitting that from the heart of a disciple comes the inner desire to not only share the salient points of her journey but provide a tool to assist others individually or in a group setting in that same discovery. Throughout the duration of her journey of faith, Barb, with open arms, has welcomed the ministry of Holy Spirit, the *paraclete* or 'One called along side to help' her in times of need, and with open invitation she invites you to that place of trust which finds one sandwiched between the hope, counsel and power of the scriptures and the person and the precise working of Holy Spirit. Join with Barb and all submitted followers as He "paddles our canoe" to completeness in Himself.

Kenn & Cheryl Gill
The Ripple Centre & Network
Calgary,   *Alberta*

Introduction

This book represents a journey through the Christian life using the image of one person's canoe expedition down a river. On this voyage, we are each the passenger and Jesus Christ is the One guiding the vessel. This journey starts with Salvation and continues through discipleship, forgiveness, trust, perseverance, relationship, patience, honour, love, joy, faith and release into ministry. Different events along the journey represent specific stages in our lives when we need to make choices, and the results are based upon the one who is paddling the canoe. In other words, who will be in control of the journey? The journey can take as long as required, or not be completed at all. The decision remains ours to make.

I have identified only a few of the stops or life-changing events that may occur along this voyage. Chosen are the most significant events within my own journey. As each of us tells our own story and reflects upon where Jesus has brought us from and where we are going, there are many more illustrations that could be added. I am trusting that my story combined with Biblical reflections may be used as an encouragement along your own personal journey.

Within each section I have also given several Scripture passages to assist with the topic. Study these verses and reflect upon the significance that each one has upon your current situation. You may have other favourite verses that the Lord gave you when you were in similar situations, and I would encourage you to note them within these pages as they come to mind.

Salvation:
Getting into the Canoe

As the journey begins, the canoe is tied to the shore in a secluded cove. You have asked Jesus into your heart and he is inviting you to join him in the canoe.

When you step into the canoe, it is just you and he; nobody else is in the boat and you have him all to yourself. The courtship has begun. You feel very safe and you realize that Jesus has chosen you. You are in love with the Lord. Your home, your family and familiar surroundings are all around you and Jesus is there, too. However, whenever you choose to, you can leave Jesus in the canoe and return to your family and friends. You may even keep your relationship with Jesus secret and lead a double life. Part of your life is spent with Jesus in the canoe that is tied to the shore, while the other part of your life leaves Jesus behind as you enjoy your current lifestyle with your friends and loved ones.

Eventually, each one of us needs to make a choice. We may make the choice willingly or Jesus may allow something to occur in our lives that will prompt us into action. For example, Jesus may allow one of our loved ones to leave us, reject us, or possibly even to die. Our health may deteriorate. We may experience financial or legal hardships, causing us to run back to the canoe to seek the Lord for explanations and reassurance or guidance. On the other hand, a person may willingly choose to abandon their former lifestyle in order to rest in the Lord always. They are prepared to "jump in with both feet."

Have you ever tried to stand up in a canoe with one foot on the shore and one foot inside the boat? It's not very stable, is it? If you do not quickly make a choice to get in or stay out, the canoe will flip over. The result— you will fall out and get very wet. You cannot continue to have a foot in each place. Perhaps during this period of instability, you reluctantly sat down, only to discover that the canoe had moved far from the shore in a mere moment of time.

Regardless of which of these people you are, the time will come when Jesus will untie the canoe and begin to paddle away from the shore. "But wait!" you say, "I want both you, Lord, and what is on the shore. I do not want to be away from those who are on the shore." You try to take the paddles from him so that you can go back.

My Story

My salvation experience was a total commitment—I chose to sit down in the canoe. To leave one foot in the canoe and one foot on the shore never crossed my mind. As you read my story you will understand why there was never any temptation to turn back. Neither did I have regret that I had fully embraced becoming a true follower of Jesus Christ.

At the age of 30, with a 3-year-old son, I realized that a second attempt to reconcile my marriage was proving to be unsuccessful. Neither my husband nor I had changed during our prior twelve-month separation. I was still battling depression and alcohol and drug dependency and he was still losing himself with his work and 'boy's nights out.' I was living in a city where there was high unemployment and limited opportunities for me to continue my professional accounting career. I was relying heavily on social events with significant alcohol consumption to allow me to escape from reality.

Although I had married into a strong Irish Catholic family, church attendance was sporadic, and usually reserved for special events only. One Sunday I reached out in desperation and attended a nearby church. One hour later, as I was walking home, I cried out, "God, where are you? I went into your church but you were not there. I am asking to be rescued and you are nowhere to be found."

That afternoon, while my young son was taking a nap and my husband was out with friends, I sat at our kitchen table and pondered the choices that were before me. Our attempts at reconciliation had failed. Counselling sessions, and there had been many (especially for me), had also led us nowhere. It was inevitable. The best decision would be to break up for good.

"Where will I go?" I pondered. Living in this city as a single parent would be unwise, for I had been unable to find a job. Maybe I should move further west? I had always wanted to live there. With relatives there, I knew that I would have temporary accommodations. However, in the early eighties, that predominantly oil and gas industry city was suffering a downturn and their employment situation would be even worse than where I currently was. I could move closer to home, I thought. That would keep me near my parents and my siblings, which would provide good family support. But no, my family still appeared to be a bit dysfunctional since my father's second wife had recently walked out on him. Although my hometown seemed secure, this was not the place for a fresh start.

"Well then, I will return to eastern Canada," I concluded, but actually, that made absolutely no sense at all. I had already lived there for three years, one of which I spent as a single parent totally involved in the drug, party and Club Med scenes. Why would I want to go back there? I had no job and certainly no place to live and I really did not want any part of that old lifestyle again. Even so, the thoughts would not go away.

When my husband returned that evening, we had another one of our long conversations and agreed that we needed to allow our marriage to end. Who should leave the home—him or me? There was no point in him leaving because I had no job and could not afford to keep the house. He understood my need to move to another city in order to find work. Although I told him about my inclination to return east, he counselled me to stay closer to our respective families. I recognized the benefits to our son if we lived closer together, however, I needed to investigate my options.

We decided that I would arrange for a moving truck to come at the end of the month and remove my half of the family possessions. Where that moving truck was going to take me was yet to be determined. In order to put these thoughts about back east to rest, I decided to fly there with my son for a one-week period. A family that I had known for some time (she had been my son's care giver) said that we could stay with them. Throughout that week, I would try to find employment or reasonable assurance that I could find work quickly. Being the financial hub of Canada at that time, I was confident that finding work there would not be a problem. I was also convinced that during this one-week fact-finding visit I could find a place for my son and myself to live.

Up until this point, all decisions were being made rationally, albeit the logic was still a bit lacking. Then my appointment with destiny arrived. During my stay, I contacted a dear friend to arrange for a coffee visit. Considering the busyness of his schedule, his only free day would be Sunday and he advised me that he would be at church in the morning. Without hesitation, I blurted out that I would love to go to church with him. I am certain that he must have dropped the phone, because any of his previous attempts to share Jesus Christ with me had fallen on deaf ears. Now, here I was, offering myself to be his guest at church. I just knew that I knew that I knew that I was supposed to be in church that day. I knew that I had reached the bottom of the pit and I knew that, based on how my friend had previously shared, God was surely in his church.

I was so excited that Sunday morning. I still remember what I was wearing—I was all decked out in my red suit with the hat that matched. The rest is history. I was convinced that the preacher was talking directly and only to me and I wept throughout the entire service. By the time the final 'Amen' was said, I was ready to be led in the sinner's prayer. I had made a royal mess of my life. I was unemployed, had no place to live, and had a failed marriage, a reputation and a little boy to support. "God, I cannot get myself up, but I know that you can." And did he ever! Within two days, I found a place to rent, and by the time I returned home at the end of the week to complete my packing, I had several job interviews lined up.

However, I was concerned that once I told my husband that I had asked Jesus to live in my heart, he might not appreciate what this meant. I knew that God hated divorce. Maybe this would be what was required in order for our marriage to get back on the right footing. With Jesus now as my guide, I was prepared to say yes to reconciliation and no to the moving truck. Maybe this canoe was not to go anywhere. Maybe I was to hold on to the paddles and stay close to the shore.

Well, my husband barely took the time to hear my story. He was convinced that I had finally lost it. He was adamant that we not try any more. We had already tried many times and been hurt each time it failed. How could this possibly make any difference? My personal relationship with the Lord Jesus would not change anything, and he explained that my previous decision to leave was still valid and that he would help me move out.

So there I was. There was nothing left for me on the shore. There was no job, no friend, no family and certainly no loving marriage to pull me back. I could not wait to run away from that old lifestyle. I was excited about all things becoming new. "Jesus, I am jumping into the boat with both feet. The sooner this journey can begin, the sooner I shall be made whole."

Study Verses for Reflection:

Reflect upon these Bible verses. How do they relate to your own life? When you read them, do they offer you hope and encouragement?

John 3:3 *"I tell you the truth, no one can see the kingdom of God unless he is born again."*

_____

_____

_____

_____

John 3:16 *"For God so loved the world that he gave his one and only Son, that whoever believes in him shall not perish but have eternal life."*

_____

_____

_____

_____

John 15:16 *"You did not choose me, but I chose you and appointed you to go and bear fruit—fruit that will last."*

_____

_____

_____

_____

Luke 9:62 *"No one who puts his hand to the plow and looks back is fit for service in the kingdom of God."*

_____

_____

_____

_____

Revelation 3:16 *"So, because you are lukewarm— neither hot nor cold—I am about to spit you out of my mouth."*

_____

_____

_____

_____

Mark 8:34b-35 *"If anyone would come after me, he must deny himself and take up his cross and follow me. For whoever wants to save his life will lose it, but whoever loses his life for me and for the gospel will save it."*

_____

_____

_____

_____

Romans 8:28 *"And we know that in all things, God works for the good of those that love him, who have been called according to his purpose."*

_____

_____

_____

_____

Psalm 18:30a *"As for God, his way is perfect."*

_____

_____

_____

_____

Psalm 138:8 *"The Lord will fulfill his purpose for me."* *("The Lord will perfect that which concerns me."* NKJV)

_____

_____

Your Journey

We need to remember that for our true Christian journey to begin, we must leave the shore. We must accept that God loves us. He has a plan for us. He wants to bless us.

Therefore, no matter what has happened—no matter what the Lord has taken you away from or what he has taken away from you—this is God's will for this time in your life. God has called you back to him and only him. Maybe it is only for a season that these relationships will be left on the shore and later they will be returned to you. Maybe it is for a lifetime. Maybe the ones that are left on the shore represent:

- A failed marriage
- An inappropriate relationship
- A lost friendship
- The death of a parent or spouse
- The loss of a child
- The comfort of the lifestyle that we used to lead
- An inappropriate work setting
- An illegal, dishonest, deceitful or immoral business arrangement

Jesus wants us to step away from all these things that distract us. He wants to begin to have a relationship with us. To do so we must acknowledge this and hand the paddles back to him.

For Group Discussion

When you accepted Jesus into your heart, what was one of the most difficult things that the Lord asked you to walk away from?

Discipleship & Restoration:
Leaving a Restful Spot

You accept that Jesus has a plan for your life and you begin to enjoy this peaceful ride. As you begin to read his word, the Bible, you realize that Jesus is telling you all about himself. He is affirming his love for you. He is providing for you and teaching you. The romance intensifies to the point that when Jesus reaches a distant shore, you now totally trust him enough to step out of the canoe and step into this new place, a place that he must certainly have prepared for you. "This must be like heaven," you think. There is peace and not confusion. There is beauty and not ashes. Everything that had been robbed from you has been given back. You are in the fellowship of the saints, confident that you can live out the rest of your life in this place.

In order to understand who Jesus is you have begun to study the gospels. You begin a devotional lifestyle with praise, worship, prayer, fasting and studying God's word becoming routine parts of your life. By studying the life of Jesus, you are beginning to understand what it means to be one of his disciples. The journey does not seem too difficult because Jesus is still very close to you.

This place where you have stopped will certainly assist in developing your walk with Christ. You belong to a spirit-filled, Bible-believing house of worship. You have been given employment in a fantastic organization and report to the perfect boss. Your neighbourhood will be perfect for raising your family. You've been blessed with many friends, Bible study groups and prayer circles. You get to like this place very much.

Then the Lord steps back into the canoe and calls you to join him. "But wait a minute, Lord. This place is perfect. Everything that I could ever ask or hope for is right here. Every one of my needs is being met here. I am loved, surrounded by friends, and enjoying the routine and discipline in my life. Plus, the Pastor of the church that I attend is fabulous. Why do I have to leave this comfortable place?"

My Story

The first stop along my journey represents the first eighteen months of my Christian walk. I was offered a position in an international company and reported to a Christian boss. I had even discovered that a couple of my co-workers were also Christians. The large home that I had rented enabled me to obtain boarders to help defray some of the rental and utility costs. I had met a beautiful woman who quickly became not only a nanny for my son, but also a spiritual mother to me. I soon became plugged into the young adult ministry at a large church and enrolled myself in several discipleship courses. Everything was turning out much better than I had ever hoped for or imagined. God had provided such a wonderful place for me, and I was being provided for, spiritually fed, loved and encouraged. My son and I were surrounded by people who loved us.

Unfortunately, I did not heed the Lord's call when he asked me to step back into the canoe. I did not want to continue along the journey, for I was very content in my situation. Why would he possibly want me to move on? Well, knowing my determination and pride, there was only one way for the Lord to get my attention. My current walls of bliss had to come tumbling down. First, I was given notice that the home I was renting was going to be sold. If I could not afford to make the first offer, I would need to move. Secondly, my employer was downsizing their Canadian operations and I was on the "to be released" list. Thirdly, after over one year of separation from my husband, he had filed for divorce. It became obvious that I was actually in control of nothing. But wait, maybe I could take the paddles and get myself to another place along this shoreline.

I'd show them! I would get another job before my severance kicked in. I'd plead with my estranged husband not to proceed with the divorce. I would pray that my home would not sell and I would be back in control. I like change and I especially thrive on the kind that I create myself. I would get myself out of here.

Well, guess what happened? No matter what I tried, the canoe did not move. I was going nowhere. I, a fairly newborn Christian, had a nervous breakdown. Jesus had allowed all these things to happen to me so that I would fall back into the canoe—only this time without all the baggage.

For the next six months, with the help of a Christian doctor as my therapist and one of the pastors at my church to fill the role of counsellor, Jesus began to do a deep work in me. He wanted to help me unload all the baggage that I was trying to carry, all the hurts that I was trying to conceal, and all the memories that I was trying to forget. He needed some intensive one-on-one time with me, without interruptions or diversions and certainly without any excuses. I was accepted into the volunteer ministry at the local church. As a result, I began to supplement my twice-weekly afternoon counselling sessions by attending volunteers' teaching and devotionals every morning. As well, twice a week, I was welcomed as a volunteer assistant for one of the discipleship Pastors.

This became a very memorable time for me. I was totally enveloped by Jesus Christ. I was being healed on the inside and encouraged on the outside. For me, a deeper relationship with Jesus began during this time. I realized that he loved me enough to allow me to hurt. He loved me enough to discipline me. He loved me enough to bring spiritual mentors into my life that would be willing to walk with me through the many "operations" and seasons of recovery.

After this time of deep inner healing (a real spiritual spa!), I sat back up in the canoe. The scenery was much different, in fact, not familiar at all. With Jesus paddling during this time, we had certainly come a long way. The previously comfortable shore was but a distant blur on the horizon behind us. I began to realize that all things could become new. The old was gone.

Study Verses for Reflection:

Reflect upon these Bible verses. How do they relate to your own life? When you read them, do they offer you hope and encouragement?

A. DISCIPLESHIP

John 8:31b-32 *"If you hold to my teaching, you are really my disciples. Then you will know the truth and the truth will set you free."*

_____

_____

_____

_____

John 15: 1-6a *"I am the true vine and my Father is the gardener. ... Remain in me, and I will remain in you. No branch can bear fruit by itself; it must remain in the vine."*

_____

_____

_____

_____

John 10:27 *"My sheep listen to my voice; I know them, and they follow me."*

_____

_____

_____

_____

Matthew 5:2b-3 *"His disciples came to him, and he began to teach them, saying, 'Blessed are the poor in spirit, for theirs is the kingdom of heaven.'"*

_____

_____

_____

_____

Hebrews 5: 13-14 *"Anyone who lives on milk, being still an infant, is not acquainted with the teaching about righteousness. But solid food is for the mature, who by constant use have trained themselves to distinguish good from evil."*

_____

_____

_____

_____

B. RESTORATION

Joel 2:25-26a *"I will repay you for the years the locust has eaten.... You will have plenty to eat..."*

_____

_____

_____

_____

Isaiah 54: 4a-6 *"You will forget the shame of your youth and remember no more the reproach of your widowhood...For your Maker is you husband—the Lord Almighty is his name...The Lord will call you back as if you were a wife deserted and distressed in spirit—a wife, who married young, only to be rejected, says your God."*

_____

_____

_____

_____

16

Isaiah 61:2-3 *"...to comfort all who mourn and provide for those who grieve in Zion—to bestow on them a crown of beauty instead of ashes, the oil of gladness instead of mourning, and a garment of praise instead of a spirit of despair."*

_____

_____

_____

_____

Your Journey

In your situation, what is "this comfortable place?" What is God asking you to give up? Are you sensing his nudging? Are you possibly starting to feel a bit restless but refusing to acknowledge it? Of course, you cannot fathom a reason why you would want to leave "this place." You should be content. Everything is perfect. You believe that you have every possible blessing that the Lord could give you. In another manner of speaking, this place of comfort may represent a favourite doll or blanket that you simply cannot throw away. You cannot imagine that the Lord may have a bigger or more beautiful doll or a larger and brighter blanket for you. This place of comfort could be:

- Your place of worship
- Your circle of friends
- Your employment
- Your neighbourhood
- Living close to your family again
- Being close to your spiritual teacher

17

You fear getting back into the canoe because you are convinced that the Lord will take you to another stop that may be unfamiliar and uncomfortable. You are reluctant to give up that familiar toy because you have waited so long to get it. Knowing that your heavenly Father gave it you in the first place, you cannot comprehend why He would want you to give it up. Will you need to do without? Is it time to suffer and grieve again? What is this place that Jesus could be leading you to?

- A different Christian fellowship
- Living closer to unsaved family members
- A stretching employment situation
- A relationship with the undesirables
- Volunteering with the poor, prisoners or the hungry
- Africa?!

You realize that you need to grow. You know that the gardener needs to do some pruning and that a time of stretching is required. You can no longer be milk-fed. It is time to be weaned.

Sometimes, this does not happen willingly. In some instances, the Lord must allow the mother's milk to grow bitter in order for the babe to leave the breast and be hungry enough to move on to something else. The milk is no longer satisfying. Is the Lord trying to wean you from a comfortable situation? Do you trust that still small voice that is telling you to get back into the canoe, or does the Lord need to sour the milk so that you leave the situation out of desperation? Either way, it will happen. It will happen because God loves us too much for us to stay where we are. He wants us to be fruitful and to make disciples of all men. How can we do that if

18

the only people we are in contact with already have a relationship with him?

For Group Discussion

When was your season of intense discipleship and restoration? If you have yet to experience such a time, what are you asking God to teach you?

Forgiveness:
Stopping Along
the Shore

Once again, you acknowledge that Jesus has a plan for
your life and that all things work together for good. You
know that God has ordered your steps so you are back in
the canoe, continuing on your journey.

Despite your reservations, the canoe journey is not
difficult. The ride remains peaceful. Jesus continues to
reveal greater truths about himself, and your relationship
with him intensifies to a new level. Much inner healing
has also taken place and he is making you whole. He has
become more than a "lover" and a "friend." He is
becoming your Father, your Papa, and your Daddy. You
are comfortable sitting on his lap with your head on his
heart. You truly feel like his daughter.

When you next look up, you discover that the canoe
is no longer in the middle of the river. Instead, he is
paddling toward another shore. You see who is standing

along the shoreline and you realize that you vowed that you never wanted to see or speak to that person again. Who is this person? Did they hurt you? Abandon you? Abuse you—physically, sexually or emotionally? Did they steal from you—a relationship, possessions or did they take credit for your deeds? Are they more successful than you are? Are you jealous or envious of him or her? Or maybe he or she is involved in a lifestyle that you still internally struggle to be part of again—a temptation. Does this person or place represent that secret room of your heart that Jesus was not allowed to enter?

You cannot possibly stop along that shore. You cannot forgive that person for what they did. You cannot allow the Lord to know what is really in your heart and that you may be tempted to fall into sin if you go ashore at this point. You are convinced that if you take hold of the paddles you can avoid this situation now and hopefully forever.

My Story

Where was my shore of forgiveness? Although I have had several, I have elected to share one of the more painful (and by far the most difficult) ones. It was the stop along the shore where my father was standing. Knowing that this represents a very sensitive subject, I am compelled to share this story because it illustrates a powerful example of God's hand both in my life and in my father's life. You see, it was my eventual willingness to allow Jesus to take me to this shore of forgiveness that brought a total reconciliation and the full restoration of a very important and healthy relationship in my life.

The story began with two seventeen-year-olds in a small farming community on the Canadian prairies. My father was quite proud of the fact that I was created in the back seat of a car on my mother's seventeenth birthday. A forced marriage followed. My father frequently reminded me that if I had not been born, he would not have had to marry my mother and he would have had a glorious career. The next fifteen years were lived in poverty on a small Manitoba farm without running water.

Throughout this time, I yearned for my father's acceptance, affection and attention. I wanted an "A-plus" father and he wanted an "A-plus" daughter, but I never seemed to be good enough for him. If he ever praised me or encouraged me as a young child, I do not recall. However, as I got a little older, I finally began to receive some time and attention from my Dad. He wanted to be my teacher, of sorts.

First, he started to read to me—passages out of magazines that would arrive in the mail in brown paper wrappings. He was convinced that he should show me about sensuality and sexuality. His attempt at sex education could have been entitled "Sex and the Single Girl," because he began to teach me about the art of pleasure, the most unwholesome sort. Unfortunately, he soon began to illustrate rather than relying on the photographs. I knew this was wrong. But what does a young girl do on a Saturday night when her Mommy, sister and brother have already gone to bed and she is alone on the couch when Daddy comes from having his bath? Deep inside I wanted to say something, but whom could I tell?

Then, when I was about fourteen, one evening my father actually called me into his bedroom. Pornographic magazines were all over the floor. My dad said that he wanted to show me something. Before I knew what was happening, I was pinned underneath him on the bed. I remember him whispering close to my ear that who better to illustrate intercourse than himself, my father. Despite my desperate pleas and my constant struggles, my 90-pound frame certainly did not have the strength to push his 230-pound body off me. I do not recall what made him stop before he could culminate this incestuous act, because no one came into the room to rescue me— not in human form anyways. I have come to realize that the Holy Spirit was at work and prevented him from continuing.

However, at the same time as this was happening behind closed doors at home, one of my father's friends was starting to "role play" the art of sexual pleasure with me and my girlfriends. So you see, at a young and vulnerable age, I was introduced into the art of giving sexual pleasure. As a result, between the ages of fourteen and eighteen I led a promiscuous life. I knew what men wanted and I had been taught how to give it to them.

I was convinced that my father had stolen my innocence, my purity. His friend ensured that I never found it again. I remember as a new Christian reading the passage of Scripture, which says, "To the pure, all things are pure" (Titus 1:5). I was not pure, so how could I think of all things as pure? How could I show myself as being pure? There were too many images in my mind that where to the contrary. I was crying for purity and the restoration of innocence.

In order for Jesus to answer that cry, my first stop along the shore of forgiveness was with my father. I knew that in order for me to receive true forgiveness I must first forgive others. It was a difficult process because my mind was certainly not willing to forgive someone who I thought had taken my innocence and purity from me. I would cry out to my pastor and his wife "You do not know what he did to me!" Yet, I knew that in order for me to receive God as my spiritual Father, I had to forgive my earthly father. Without forgiveness, I would never have an "Abba Father" relationship with God. There would always be a barrier of distrust and scepticism. I believed that love came with conditions—at least that was what my earthly father had illustrated. You get an "A" and I will praise you. You let me illustrate my sexual fantasies with you, and I will shower my affections upon you.

Through prayer and fasting, counselling and the encouragement of my pastor, I was able to forgive my father. Then, upon my next trip home, which happened to be during Christmas, I arranged a visit with my father where not only did I say that I forgave him, but I asked him to forgive me for the hatred and bitterness that I had felt towards him for all these years. As you can imagine, it was not an easy conversation because my father still refused to admit what he had done or that it had been wrong. He wanted that entire season of our lives to be forgotten. However, we cannot forget without forgiveness. Even then, it is only the power of God that will allow those memories to drown in a sea of forgetfulness.

The canoe journey towards that shore of forgiveness had me grabbing for the paddles many times. It was a slow and painful process, but one that I am certainly relieved that Jesus walked me through. By stopping on the shore of forgiveness, I have become able to receive my heavenly Father's love, to trust his direction and intentions for my life, and to understand that he loves me unconditionally.

Study Verses for Reflection:

Reflect upon these Bible verses. How do they relate to your own life? When you read them, do they offer you hope and encouragement?

FORGIVENESS

Romans 8:15-17 *"For you did not receive a spirit that makes you a slave again to fear, but you received the Spirit of sonship. And by him we cry, 'Abba, Father.' The Spirit himself testifies with our spirit that we are God's children. Now, if we are children, then we are heirs—heirs of God and co-heirs with Christ, if indeed we share in his sufferings in order that we may also share in his glory."*

_____

_____

_____

_____

Ephesians 4:32 *"Be kind and compassionate to one another, forgiving each other, just as in Christ God forgave you."*

_____

_____

_____

_____

Matthew 6:14-15 *"For if you forgive men when they sin against you, your heavenly Father will also forgive you. But if you do not forgive men their sins, your Father will not forgive your sins."*

_____

_____

26

Psalm 90:8 *"You have set our iniquities before you, our secret sins in the light of your presence."*

1 Corinthians14:25a *"...and the secrets of his heart will be laid bare."*

FLEE FROM SIN

Galatians 5:19-21 *"The acts of the sinful nature are obvious: sexual immorality, impurity and debauchery; idolatry and witchcraft; hatred, discord, jealousy, fits of rage, selfish ambition, dissentions, factions and envy; drunkenness, orgies and the like. I warn you, as I did before, that those who live like this will not inherit the kingdom of God."*

Romans 6:11, 14 *"In the same way, count yourselves dead to sin but alive to God in Christ Jesus...For sin shall not be your master, because you are not under law, but under grace."*

27

_____

_____

_____

_____

Your Journey

Patiently and lovingly Jesus will show you that you must stop here. You must be healed so that you can be set free. You must forgive others so that you can experience the forgiveness that comes from the Father. Jesus already knows the secret places of your heart. He already knows what tempts you. He wants to set you free. What is this secret place? Who are you unable to forgive? What is that hidden sin?

- A father, uncle, brother who sexually abused you and stole your innocence
- A boyfriend or husband who physically abused you
- A sibling who always got what she wanted, who always did everything right; the star, the successful one, the favourite
- A boss or co-worker that picked on you, bullied you, and took glory for your work and ideas
- A friend that hurt you many years ago by leaving you out, or who took your boyfriend or husband

Or is this a secret sin?

- Promiscuity or pornography
- Obsessive-compulsive behaviour
- Depression and anxiety
- Greed, lust

Once again, you acknowledge the good and perfect plan that Jesus has for you and understand that you must deal with these issues in order to move on in health and freedom. With the Lord's help, you know that you can overcome. You give the paddles back to Jesus and allow his good and perfect will to continue in your life. You appreciate that this will be a painful experience, but, with the Lover of your soul beside you, you know that the ending will be better than the beginning. Obedience and trust continue to build a foundation.

For Group Discussion

Name one of the people that the Lord has asked you to forgive. Why was this difficult?

Trust:
Going a Different Route

After a season of tears, struggles and finally the release of all those secrets and unforgiveness, Jesus invites you back into the canoe and your journey resumes. You are feeling set free and begin to experience a deep inner joy. You believe that you are ready for whatever the Lord has for you, and as the canoe approaches a beautiful island, you are disappointed that the Lord is not stopping there. The last stop that Jesus made was a tough one, but this one could be very pleasurable—a vacation, maybe! But you have come to realize that he is in charge of the canoe and you want to trust him.

"Surely the Lord will allow us to stop here," you say to yourself. "Maybe when we get around to the other side, he will stop." You see the course that the Lord has chosen and you discover that it is away from all the beautiful scenery that the island has to offer. You take the paddles back from the Lord because you are certain that he would not mind if you made a brief stop. You are still going in the right direction. You simply want to go around the other side of the island because you are confident that you saw a shallow cove up ahead. This would be a beautiful place to rest and have a brief swim.

Suddenly, the water becomes very rough. That was not a cove that you saw. All that is ahead of you is a very narrow passage with rough water, rapids and sharp reefs. Viewing the high cliffs that have risen before you, you realize that there will be no safe shores to land upon. "Okay, Lord, I took the paddles. I can do this," you state confidently. "I can steer this canoe through the passage. I will not get hurt because I know that you are here to protect me."

But guess what happens—the canoe capsizes! Your foot gets caught in a logjam. You realize that Jesus has allowed this to happen. "Help me!" you cry. "Rescue me!" However, it may not be the Lord's hand that reaches down and picks you up. This time he may use a brother or sister in the Lord. The Lord remains nearby, but he wants you to learn a lesson. You cannot tempt him, and you cannot succeed without the accountability and the fellowship of the Christian people who have been called to edify you daily.

My Story

When I reflect upon the added dimension that being saved at age thirty brings, the last eighteen years of my Christian journey have had a few bumpy direction changes. There have been a few points where I fell out of the canoe and got caught in a logjam. Probably one of the most impacting experiences occurred when I fell out of the boat while I was pursuing an ungodly relationship with an unsaved man.

It was 1990, and I had just completed a three-week short-term mission trip to Eastern and Western Europe. The team had returned to Canada and I was about to spend another two weeks traveling through Europe—the vacation of a lifetime. Anyone who has been on any form of mission excursion will know that we are the most vulnerable once the outreach has finished. I was travelling alone with limited accountability and, you guessed it, I was like a sitting duck. Satan came in like a flood. I was vulnerable and he knew it. The curious thing was that I did not even try to avoid the rapids.

The story unfolded at the first stop in my travels, Baden-Baden Germany, beside a Christian friend's swimming pool. She, a German, and her new boyfriend, a member of the Canadian armed forces, had arranged for another gentleman to join us for a swim and a late dinner. What walked into the yard that late afternoon was nothing short of an Adonis. He was over 6 feet tall, dark, tanned and in excellent physical shape. One look into his deep brown eyes and I knew that I would be toast. "I can do this, Lord," I thought. "I may be a 35-year-old divorcee, but I am a strong Christian and I will not give in to these thoughts. I have two Christians with me to whom I can give my attention. If I do not look his way, I shall not succumb to the temptation that lies within and I shall be able to handle these next three days of visiting without falling into the rapids."

Well, evening #1 was a success and day and evening #2 were victorious as well. It was the afternoon and evening of day #3 that finally saw me fall overboard. Not only had I looked into his eyes, but I had totally fallen for him. Without much quarrel, I agreed to stay in his flat prior to leaving for Switzerland the next morning. I had convinced myself that since he lived only a block from the train station, it would be less inconvenient than for my friends to have to drive me into town early the next morning. Satan was persistent and I was slowly falling into his trap.

The enemy had his foothold and over the course of the next eighteen months we carried out a long-distance love affair. I returned to Germany twice and he came back to Canada once so that we could be together. I knew that he was not a Christian and had no desire to become one. I also knew that my own walk was being compromised. However, I willingly allowed passion to overrule the practical. I would get so annoyed when well-meaning Christian sisters would invade my privacy and question my intentions. They even tried to rebuke my actions. I elected to keep most of the relationship a secret and never bothered to admit what was actually transpiring. "I can handle this," I thought, "my foot might be stuck, but I shall not drown."

Finally, through the constant prayers of some very good friends (remember, better is the rebuke from a friend than the kisses of an enemy), my eyes were opened and I began to see the situation for what it really was. Satan had his agents out to see my downfall. I was being emotionally and spiritually destroyed. Everything that Jesus had healed and delivered me from, especially all the lust of sexual sin, was flooding back into my life. Satan would constantly remind me of my past and tell me that I would never change. I was promiscuous as a teenager and young adult, and he wanted me to believe that I would be promiscuous until I died.

Through the love and faithfulness of my friends and many subsequent trips to the altar, I knew that God remained faithful to forgive all my sins. I only had to ask. I was a new creation. All things had again become new. I needed to remember that when Satan reminded me of my past, I needed to remind him of his future. I was a child of the King, and no weapon, no device of the enemy, would prosper against me.

Study Verses for Reflection:

Reflect upon these Bible verses. How do they relate to your own life? When you read them, do they offer you hope and encouragement?

Luke 4:12 *"Jesus answered, 'It says: "Do not put the Lord your God to the test."'"*

_____

_____

_____

_____

Proverbs 3:5 *"Trust in the Lord and lean not on your own understanding; in all your ways acknowledge him, and he will make your paths straight."*

_____

_____

_____

_____

Hebrews 12:4-6 *"In your struggle against sin, you have not yet resisted to the point of shedding your blood. And you have forgotten that word of encouragement that addresses you as sons: "My son, do not make light of the Lord's discipline, and do not lose heart when he rebukes you, because the Lord disciplines those he loves and he punishes everyone he accepts as a son."*

_____

_____

2 Timothy 4:2 *"Preach the Word; be prepared in season and out of season; correct, rebuke and encourage—with great patience and careful instruction."*

Proverbs 27:5 *"Better is open rebuke than hidden love."*

Psalm 62:8 *"Trust in him at all times..."*

Jeremiah 7:4 *"Do not trust in deceptive words..."*

Ezekiel 33 – read the entire chapter

Your Journey

Where are you having difficulty trusting the Lord? Do you feel that He has let you down? You used to say that you trusted God but He did not make the path straight. In a time of anger or rebellion, you said, "Okay, I am 'checking out' for awhile. I'll catch up with Him later."

Maybe these difficult paths or times of testing have resulted in you embarking in one of the following areas:

- An ungodly relationship
- The consistent pursuit of the wrong career
- A "my way" attitude of planning your life
- A circle of friends who always seem to be placing temptations in front of you that you have trouble resisting
- An insistence upon gaining more and more material possessions

God may allow us to do things our own way for a time. He may allow us to test him for a time. But remember, the Bible says that we must be either hot or cold. God will spew the lukewarm Christian out of his mouth. If you are in a time of rebellion and walking through life with a stubborn, non-surrendered attitude, you must stop and reconsider the future consequences of your actions. God's path may not be straightforward. He may lead us down before he can take us up, but we must trust in Him. In all our ways, whether in our relationships, our families, our careers, our finances or our possessions, we must acknowledge him. You know what happens after that—He promises to give us the desires of our hearts! The key is to trust him. We cannot go through life resting on our feelings, our logic or our reasoning. God expects us to walk in faith.

Do not worry. In all your ways acknowledge Jesus and he will make your paths straight. He will put you back on the right course. If you have fallen out of the boat, confess your mistake (your sin), and God will be faithful to forgive you, pull you out of the water and set your feet back upon solid ground.

For Group Discussion

What areas of your life do you believe that you have given over to the Lord? Were the results different then when you tried your own way?

Perseverance:
Learning to Paddle the Canoe

You have now been lifted back into the canoe and have had a chance to dry off. The rough waters have subsided into a fast moving river, and the journey continues to be turbulent.

Jesus, knowing your eagerness to assist in the journey, allows you to take up a paddle. He has given you permission to paddle alongside him. This seems quite easy at the start. However, after many hours of the constant rhythm of dipping your paddle into the water, pulling back, lifting up out of the water and starting again, you become very tired. "Oh Lord, I cannot go on. My arms are weary, my body is weak and I'm thirsty. Can we rest awhile so that I may eat to regain my energy? May I have a drink of water?" Jesus agrees to the rest because he knows that you will need your energy for what is to come. You, however, are presuming that there will be no more rough waters and that your journey will resume the way it was—nice and peaceful, tranquil water, birds singing, the sun shining, a slight breeze and Jesus doing all the work.

The rest does not last long. After some brief refreshments and a nap, Jesus nudges you and urges you to take up the paddle again. He explains that the canoe is about to enter an area of rapids and it is very important that you follow his lead and paddle through the chutes that are up ahead. "No problem!" you exclaim. "I have had a rest. Plus with you by my side, instructing me all the way, I am ready for whatever is ahead."

I don't know if you have had the opportunity to experience white water rafting. I have gone twice and have come to appreciate the advice and expertise of the guides. Firstly, there will always be more than one set of rapids that you must manoeuvre through. Secondly, the first one is never the hardest one. Thirdly, if you do not heed the call of the guide and paddle for all you're worth, the raft will either tip over, crash upon the rocks or become caught in a whirlpool.

So there you are. You've just successfully navigated three serious sets of rapids and Jesus alerts you to prepare for the one around the corner. There is a sharp drop in the middle of the rapids and it is important that you lean forward into the direction that the raft is going. If you let up or lean back, the raft will capsize and all will be lost.

My Story

When (during the eighteen years of my Christian walk) have I most needed perseverance? When has my journey been the most challenging or difficult to endure?

Most of my employment situations have been one step beyond what I have been comfortable handling, which meant that I had to rely on the strength and wisdom of Jesus to get me through each day. In one particular company, I had a very demanding, domineering and controlling boss. Since he was a perfectionist, I soon discovered that he would always recheck everything I did and that regardless of how hard I tried, he would always find something to correct. No matter what I did, he would redo it, and as a result my self-esteem and confidence began to decrease rapidly. Restless Sunday nights would become anxious Monday mornings. I decided that, for sanity's sake, I needed to take some control of my life and find other employment. Given my credentials, it was not long before I was being interviewed for a comparable position a little closer to home. However, when the job offer came, I did not have that overwhelming joyful feeling. I was hesitant and could not understand why. I had wanted out of the company and I had found another job, so why did I not have any peace about moving on?

Through the aid of prayer and my devotional reading, the Lord began to lead me through some of Paul's journeys. One particular voyage that Paul took ministered to me greatly. In the book of Acts, chapter 27, Paul was a prisoner on a ship that was taking him to Rome. The captain of the ship was advised to winter in a place called Fairhaven, however, he refused to listen. Instead, the ship continued on their journey, got caught in a hurricane and became shipwrecked on the island of Malta. None of the crew or prisoners were lost throughout this ordeal. After spending time in Malta waiting for better weather, they continued on to Rome and Paul arrived there safely.

This passage ministered to me immensely, for you see, no matter which course was taken, no matter whether they wintered in Fairhaven or in Malta, Paul would still arrive at his destination—Rome. The Lord had said that it would be better if Paul and company had wintered in Fairhaven. To me, this meant that it would be better for me to winter at my current position. Certainly God would allow me to leave and I would be granted fair weather for a while. However, if I left, I would become ship wrecked. Yes, I would still arrive at his ultimate destination for me but not through his preferred plan. This meant that I had to persevere. So persevere I did. The winter lasted more than the three-month season that may have been expected. Rather, it lasted about a year. Through that year, God allowed me to witness to many more people and actually lead a fellow co-worker to Christ. He was instrumental in using me to disciple her as well as be her friend through her very difficult marriage break up.

There were also times when endurance was required with the raising of my eldest son. During my years as a single parent he was a model son and not tempted to be part of the wrong crowd, do drugs or drop out of school. Even though there was still an estranged father entering the scene from time to time, conflict was minimal. After I had been remarried for eighteen months and given birth to another child, my son, at the age of thirteen, asked if he could go and live with his natural father. To grant his request would mean his moving to another city and attending a different school for grade eight, a challenging time in any adolescent's life. We agreed that he could go, providing that he committed to stay a full year and that by the end of that year he would need to decide where he wanted to remain. Once his school year was completed, he would have to decide whether he wished to stay with his father and stepmother for the remainder of his schooling or if he wanted to return to his mother and stepfather.

Throughout that year I had no idea if he was going to choose to come back when the time was finished or if he would choose to stay. I had to persevere, believing that no matter what happened, he would remain in God's will. However, God, in his faithfulness, had given me Scripture verses that would help carry me through. Time and time again, I was directed to the book of Philemon. Onesimus would leave and it was expedient that he should do so, but after a time, he would return. I trusted God that after a time my son would return. I only had to persevere.

Shortly after receiving a peace about my son's departure to live with his father, my second husband returned from work stating that he was soon leaving on a U.N. peacekeeping tour to Croatia. "Okay Lord, I can handle this," I thought. Well, he had barely left on the plane when I was served with legal papers from my ex-husband, who now wanted me to provide child support to him while our son was living with him. The tables had certainly turned. I had been prepared to forfeit the payments that I had been receiving while our son was living with us, but now to have to pay him? I was taken completely by surprise.

I shall never forget sitting at my kitchen table, tears of defeat running down my cheeks as our new one-year-old son watched from his high chair. It was not long before I was reminded of a time ten years before. Was this deja vu? "Lord, did I not learn everything the first time around? Here I am, effectively a single mom again with a baby to care for because my husband cannot be here to help me. Why do I have to do this all over again?" Well, after the tears had ceased and I took a deep breath, I stood up, gave my baby a hug and determined in my spirit that with the grace of God, I could preserve through this experience one more time. Working full time, daily home routines, flat tires, the croup, winter storms, legal battles and trying to balance the family budget could all be accomplished if I remembered to lean on Jesus. I am not going to say that everything was rosy during my husband's tour of duty. There were times when it seemed the clock stood still, but we persevered. We made it through—one day at a time.

As you may suspect, another test of endurance came at about eight years into my current marriage. After being a single mother for seven years, the Lord had released me to marry a wonderful Christian man who had also been previously divorced. We were living in our city of choice in a home that we had recently built. But all was not rosy. Even though we voluntarily took a Marital Improvement course entitled "His Needs, Her Needs," our daily lives were in conflict. If this was married bliss, did we want any more part of it?

One evening my husband announced that he did not want to be married anymore. Within seconds, my emotions went from anger to obstinacy and stubbornness. I wanted to say, "Fine! When are you moving out?" and then I thought, "No way, I shall kick you out and you will take nothing." Finally I said out loud, "Oh, no you are not! You cannot just say that you do not want to be married any longer and that you are going to begin making a new life for yourself. Either you are in or you are out. If you stay living in this home, then you need to know that I will continue to love you as my husband and treat you as the father to our sons. There is no way that the devil is going to win!"

The fact that he never walked out, but stayed living in our home, meant that he would continue to witness my daily walk. Well, if I ever needed to be Christ-like, now was the time. The armies of heaven would be with me and around him whenever he was home. Just think, if he had moved out, God could not have used me as effectively. But instead, he was right there beside me. I prayed. I fasted. I asked the Lord to help me live 1 Peter 3:1-2 every day: "...they may be won over without talk by the behaviour of their wives, when they see the purity and reverence of your lives." I held on to God's word that my husband's life would be changed through the example that I lived, and perseverance paid off. Three months later, he finally said that he did not know what had come over him. He wanted to be married and asked me to forgive him for the difficulties that the past few months had caused. Perseverance paid off. I had to die daily to my own free, stubborn and obstinate will and hold on to the word that God hates divorce. The enemy was not going to gain a further foothold into our family. With me and my God, we were the majority, and through perseverance, we would be victorious.

Study Verses for Reflection:

Reflect upon these Bible verses. How do they relate to your own life? When you read them, do they offer you hope and encouragement?

Romans 5:3-4 *"Not only so, but we also rejoice in our sufferings; because we know that suffering produces perseverance; perseverance, character; and character, hope."*

_____

_____

_____

_____

Hebrews 12:1, 3 *"Therefore, since we are surrounded my such a great cloud of witnesses, let us throw off everything that hinders and the sin that so easily entangles, and let us run with perseverance the race marked out for us...Consider him who endured such opposition from sinful men, so that you will not grow weary and lose heart."*

_____

_____

_____

_____

James 1:2-4 *"Consider it pure joy, my brothers, whenever you face trials of many kinds, because you know that the testing of your faith develops perseverance. Perseverance must finish its work so that you may be mature and complete..."*

_____

_____

_____

_____

1Timothy 4:16 *"Watch your life and doctrine closely. Persevere in them, because if you do, you will save both yourself and your hearers."*

_____

_____

_____

_____

Hebrews 10:36 -39 *"You need to persevere so that when you have done the will of God, you will receive what he has promised. For in just a very little while, 'He who is coming will come and will not delay. But my righteousness one will live by faith. And if he shrinks back, I will not be pleased with him.' But we are not of those who shrink back and are destroyed, but of those who believe and are saved."*

_____

James 5:11a *"As you know, we consider blessed those who have persevered."*

_____

1 Corinthians 13:6-7 *"Love does not delight in evil but rejoices with the truth. It always protects, always trusts, always hopes, always perseveres."*

_____

Isaiah 41:10b *"...I will strengthen you and help you; I will uphold you with my righteous right hand."*

_____

Philippians 4:13 *"I can do everything through him who gives me strength."*

_____

_____

_____

_____

Your Journey

Are you trying to persevere through a season that you created because you did not take time to rest when you were told? What has caused you to become weary and unrested? Why are you tired? Have you been too tired to pray? Are you too exhausted to spend time with your loved ones? Is all your energy being spent in the wrong places? Can you relate to few of these scenarios?

- Being a successful business person who works over fifty hours per week
- Caring for three children, each involved in dance, hockey and swimming, respectively
- Having a spouse who travels
- Volunteering on one too many boards
- Volunteering at your children's school
- Driving your elderly parents to their doctor's appointments
- Teaching Sunday School
- Being a community or political advocate

Are you being asked to persevere during a time you were confident that you had been prepared and trained for? In this second scenario, you are shooting the rapids with Jesus, just as you had planned. You thought that you had experienced the worst but have just been advised that the most difficult challenge is ahead of you. You are weary from all of the paddling and doubt that you can continue. Maybe this represents a series of mishaps and misfortunes that have fallen upon you.

- You lose your job
- One of your parents has recently been diagnosed with Alzheimer's and your siblings have agreed that you are the most likely candidate for fulfilling the care-giving role.
- Your teenage daughter tells you that she is pregnant
- You discover that your adolescent son has been caught selling drugs
- Your spouse confesses to an affair
- You've been diagnosed with cancer

No matter what situation we find ourselves in, we must seek the Lord's guidance. If it is time to rest, then he will tell us so. If we need to persevere, Scripture verses shall come to mind to strengthen us.

For Group Discussion

During your Christian walk, what has been one of the most difficult challenges that you have had to endure? How did Jesus help you through this time?

Relationship:
Taking on Other
Passengers

There will be other seasons in this journey when there will be more than just you and Jesus in the boat. Sometimes, along the way, the Lord will ask you to reach overboard and pull someone else into the canoe with you. Not only has the Lord rescued you, but he also wants to use you, unselfishly, to rescue others. This is no time for self-centeredness or greed. During this season, God will break the back of both of these attributes. When you consider your journey, it becomes very apparent that as long as there is only you and the Lord every day, you find that you can make it. It's when other people come across our paths that we become impatient, easily angered, judgemental, envious, jealous and much more. Yet, we need each other in order to move closer in our relationship with Jesus. "How can relationships help me to become closer to Jesus?" you ponder.

Firstly, difficult relationships will cause us to get on our knees and ask for guidance, wisdom and understanding. It is through these difficult relationships that we realize that without the Lord's help every day, we cannot continue on. We cannot minister love without the love of the Father. How can we exercise pure religion if we do not extend our hands to the poor, feed the hungry, or look after the widow and the orphan in their distress? All of these actions require relationship. We need to use our hands to touch somebody else's life.

In your Christian walk you cannot merely pick and choose those whom we want to associate with. Many times the Lord will purposefully bring others along your path so that you have a choice as to whether or not you will reach out to them. These people could be the street person, the rough co-worker, the dependent family member or the stranger on the side of the road or that difficult next-door neighbour. Jesus wants you to get wet and dirty, too. There are people in the water that need rescuing. You are their life preserver with the rope that pulls them into the boat. Now is the time for you to reach out and clothe them, feed them, love them and yes, even hug them. You must adopt them into your family. You must invite them into your home. You must pray for them.

My Story

When I first became a Christian, making decisions about my relationships was very simple. Within a matter of months, I ensured that I was surrounded by Christian brothers and sisters who would encourage me and lead me into the paths of righteousness. I wanted accountability and I wanted to make certain that I was not around anyone who would cause me to fall. However, as I began to mature, I noticed that the Lord began to put other people into my path that I had a choice to befriend. When I think back upon three women in particular, one similar threads shows up in each story. When God asked me to reach over the side of the boat and help pull somebody inside, I was emotionally at my lowest. I could barely care for my own needs and work out my own salvation, let alone give of myself to someone else. Yet, I knew that God wanted me to reach out. In all three situations, the reaching began in my marketplace—the places where I worked.

The first experience occurred while I was working at a healthcare facility. A consultant from the local accounting office was helping us with some tax work. When we took a moment for lunch, I quickly discovered that she was at a crossroads in her career and in her life in general. With mixed emotions, sprinkled with a lot of fear and insecurity, I shared how I had been able to make a decision when I was at my crossroads in life. I shared my testimony, and before I could comprehend what I was doing, I realized that I had opened up myself and shared part of my spiritual journey to a near stranger, and a businesswoman, at that! What was she thinking as I shared about my faith?

As the conversation progressed, her interest grew and she began to ask many questions. Before the lunch was finished, she acknowledged that she had not been to church for quite some time and needed to go back. Well, she honoured her word. Not only did she and her family return to church, but she also recommitted her life to Christ, and began her own Bible study and prayer group at her new place of work. Since then, she has received her Masters of Divinity and is now involved in full time ministry. Look at the seed that God had me watering— simply through relationship!

A second lady's story began at another workplace. I had tried desperately to move on to greener pastures, but the Lord had not released me. Then, one spring, I was asked to share my testimony at a Women's Ministry meeting. I got up enough courage to prepare some announcements and used them to invite all my female co-workers. Unfortunately, none of them came to the church that evening. However, one lady was very appreciative that I had even considered asking her. As a result, a window of opportunity to communicate had opened. Again, once I had managed to overcome the fear and gain courage, I asked if she would be willing to come to church with me as we were having a special speaker over several nights and the messages were excellent. I was confident that she would be encouraged.

Well, she came and she committed her life to the Lord. The next eighteen months began a serious time of ministry and discipleship for her. As she leaned on me for teaching, guidance and support, I leaned on the Lord for answers and for strength. The Lord used me to get her into the word and encourage her to become a faithful attendee at weekly Bible studies. After a time, our lives took us on to different paths. I am no longer aware of where she is and how her walk with the Lord is. However, I do know that she knows the truth. She knows the way and she is now accountable to ensure that she walks in that truth.

The last story that I will share involves another lady in a more recent place of work. Shortly after I had arrived at my new job, I began meeting with each of my subordinates to find out more about them—what their positions were, their strengths and the challenges that they faced with their job tasks. One woman was quite forthright about her personal situation. She risked a lot that day by advising me that she would be leaving early from time to time because she was getting some counselling. I thanked her for her honesty. Then, before I realized what was happening, I remarked that counselling was an excellent way of getting to the root of issues that affect our behaviour, but that without Jesus to be there to heal what we dug up, we would never see the wounds go away. She indicated that she was not ready to walk on that path. I assured her that if she ever changed her mind, I would welcome her to attend church with me.

Over the next several months, as we continued to work together, I would encourage her every opportunity that I could. About eighteen months after we had met, she asked to see me in my office one day. To my complete surprise, she asked if she could come to church with me the upcoming Sunday. I gladly confirmed my invitation and arranged to pick her up. Not only did I witness this "hardened street-smart" woman giving her heart to the Lord that night, but I have watched her mature over the past few years. She is hungry for the things of God, disciplined in the word and faithful in her prayer walk. She has been on a short-term mission trip and is seriously considering more permanent forms of overseas ministry opportunities.

There are many more stories that I could share. The Lord has asked me to reach outside of my comfort zone on many occasions. Some individuals have gotten into the canoe with me and worked out their salvation as they have journeyed along the river with me. Others have held my hand on the outside of the boat, refusing to get in, and there have been many others who have wanted no part of the canoe ride. In these cases, I say, "Thank-you Lord for giving me the opportunity of touching their lives. May my life be a testimony and my actions an example that will lead them along their own paths of salvation." May I never say that that another canoe behind me will pick them up when I know that God has asked me to do the reaching!

Study Verses for Reflection:

Reflect upon these Bible verses. How do they relate to your own life? When you read them, do they offer you hope and encouragement?

Proverbs 27:17 *"As iron sharpens iron, so one man sharpens another."*

_____

_____

_____

_____

Ecclesiastes 4:9-10 *"Two are better than one, because they have a good return for their work: If one falls down, his friend can help him up. But pity the man who falls and has no one to help him up!"*

_____

_____

_____

_____

John 15:13 *"Greater love has no one that this, that he lay down his life for his friends."*

_____

_____

_____

_____

Matthew 27:55 *"Many women were there, watching from a distance. They had followed Jesus from Galilee to care for his needs."*

_____

_____

_____

_____

Romans 16:4 *"They risked their lives for me. Not only I but all the churches of the Gentiles are grateful to them."*

_____

_____

_____

_____

Acts 2:42 *"They devoted themselves to the apostles' teaching and to the fellowship, to the breaking of bread and to prayer."*

_____

_____

_____

_____

Isaiah 54:10 *" 'Though the mountains be shaken and the hills be removed, yet my unfailing love for you will not be shaken nor my covenant of peace be removed,' says the Lord, who has compassion on you."*

_____

_____

_____

_____

Micah 6:8 *"He has showed you, O Man, what is good. And what does the Lord require of you? To act justly and to love mercy and to walk humbly with your God."*

_____

_____

_____

_____

James 1:27 *"Religion that God our Father accepts as pure and faultless is this: to look after orphans and widows in their distress and to keep oneself from being polluted by the world."*

_____

_____

_____

_____

Your Journey

Are you in a place of contentment in your walk with the Lord? As long as there is just you and your Jesus, are you fine? Possibly you've considered becoming a monk or a nun so that you could devote your life to fasting and prayer and remove all the busy distractions from your life, and yet, that is not what the Lord has called all of us to. We are to be in fellowship with one another. Without each other, who would encourage us? Who could we encourage? Who would bless us? How could we bless others? Who could heal our hurts? Who could comfort our sufferings? Without relationships, we could not be the Lord's hands in action. We could not comfort those who mourn, or laugh with those who are joyful. We would have no one to share our life's entire journey with.

Remember, the Lord made us male and female so that we could be helpmates and friends to one another—the sacrament of marriage requires two people in a relationship. Jesus also sent his disciples out in pairs. We need our relationships with one another in order to fully understand our relationship with the Father, the Son and the Holy Spirit.

Have you looked over the side of the canoe? There are drowning people all around you crying out to be rescued. Are you afraid that if you reach out your hand, they will pull you overboard and you will fall into the murky water? Although the canoe is very easily tipped, do not worry about falling in. Remember, Jesus is in the canoe holding onto you so that when someone grabs your extended arm, He will help you pull them in. The canoe will not tip over.

When the Lord asks you to reach outside your comfort zone and offer something of yourself to someone else, please be obedient. Remember, God's word says that obedience is better than sacrifice. In my own life one of the most powerful scriptures that illustrates obedience is Matthew 25:35-16: "For I was hungry and you gave me something to eat, I was thirsty and you gave me something to drink, I was a stranger and you invited me in, I needed clothes and you clothed me, I was sick and you looked after me, I was in prison and you came to visit me."

For Group Discussion

When you reached out and helped someone, how did you feel? Did Jesus have to prompt you more than once?

Patience:
Wanting to
Paddle Faster

You have persevered and the Lord has permitted you to enter another season of rest. After a time, you think to yourself, "The canoe must surely be approaching its destination now." As you contemplate for a moment, you look up to see a beautiful ocean expanse before you. You cannot wait to get there. The earlier visions that the Lord shared with you come back into your remembrance. The desires of your heart, which represent all of your dreams, are right there ahead of you—just beyond your reach. You know that this is God's purpose for your life and you want to get to it.

Although the current within the river is allowing the canoe to move faster than it had before, Jesus has stopped paddling. "Why will he not paddle?" you think. "Lord, you know that these are the desires of my heart. If you paddled, we would get there so much quicker.

Can't you see that the lost are perishing, the hungry need to be fed and the poor need to be clothed? These people are dying. They need to hear the gospel, now, Lord!" Jesus seems unmoved by your anxiousness, but this is not acceptable to you. Therefore, you pick up the oar and start to paddle. You believe that if you work along with the current, you will arrive at the destination sooner and the ministry that you have been called to can begin.

For some reason, the canoe is not moving any faster along the river. If anything, it seems to be going around in circles. Your paddling has countered the effect of the current. In frustration, or possibly even in simple zealousness, you abandon the paddle and jump into the river. You can swim the rest of the way—it is not that far.

After exerting all your energy, you discover that you are still too far away from the destination. It was much further than you estimated. You look behind you and the canoe is also very far away. "Oh Lord!" you cry. "Help me! I cannot go on and it is too far for me to come back. Lord, please rescue me." Once again, in His miraculous way, Jesus is right beside you. He reaches over the side of the canoe and lifts your dripping, aching body back inside.

My Story

I admire people that are content and demonstrate the kind of patience that just oozes out of them every time they talk. I used to think that these people were the wonderful mothers; the soft-spoken, submissive wives who were always content in all that life seemed to offer them. That was certainly not me. I was driven—the assertive type. One well-meaning pastor even said, "Beware of Barbara, she always gets what she wants." Now, in one way, this is good. It shows vision, determination, and the ability to set goals, plans and priorities. Not only was I an esteemed visionary, but I could also be strategic and tactical in ensuring that those dreams were fulfilled. Unfortunately, I may not have demonstrated patience along the way.

One story that illustrates my lack of patience and my willingness to try another way in order to achieve what I was certain the Lord wanted would be my involvement within a parachurch organization. I was convinced that I was to be involved in ministry somehow. I had created a "Vision to Volunteer" proposal for our local church that would see me come on staff, give them all my expertise and then leave after they had gleaned all that I had to offer. I could be the "White Knight." Everything that I had learned and everything that I had become could be used for God's glory to help the church business office become more proficient and professional. Well, nothing materialized in that venue, so I entertained the possibility of becoming involved at the grass roots level of another Christian organization that was starting. I had originally been asked to become involved at a governance and advisory level at the inception of their vision, and I was passionate about what they were doing and saw all the groundbreaking work that needed to be done. However, I also believed that the timing was right for me to move on from my current job. If you recall, my previously referenced season entitled "Winter in Fairhaven" was coming to a close. Rather than be on the Council, I thought I could become one of their employees, and I was certain that God could really use me.

Well, just as I had planned, the staff position was offered to me. However, shortly after accepting, I began to realize that this was not what the Lord had for me at all. I had grabbed the paddles and had tried to rush God.

Fortunately, I was able to reconsider and refuse the offer before it was too late. But the damage had been done. My hastiness and lack of patience had allowed me to be involved in areas that God did not want me to be part of. I saw many ungodly things and non-God-fearing actions occur within that Christian work setting. Unfortunately, my lack of maturity made it very difficult for me to process what I saw without being judgemental. The good news was that I was able to gracefully leave this environment and subsequently resign from their Board of governance. However, a root of bitterness and disappointment had set in and it would take many months for these wounds to heal. God had to take me through another walk of forgiveness. I had to learn the meaning of mercy and realize that all of us fall short of the glory of God. I had to take the plank out of my own eye before I could judge the speck that was in my co-workers' eyes.

Study Verses for Reflection:

Reflect upon these Bible verses. How do they relate to your own life? When you read them, do they offer you hope and encouragement?

Colossians 1:10-11 *"And we pray this in order that you may live a life worthy of the Lord and may please him in every way: bearing fruit in every good work, growing in knowledge of God, being strengthened will all power according to his glorious might so that you may have great endurance and patience..."*

_____
_____
_____
_____

2 Timothy 4:2 *"Preach the Word; be prepared in season and out of season; correct, rebuke and encourage—with great patience and careful instruction."*

_____

_____

_____

_____

Proverbs 14:29a *"A patient man has great understanding..."*

_____

_____

_____

_____

Proverbs 16:32a *"Better a patient man than a warrior..."*

_____

_____

_____

_____

James 5:8 *"You, too, be patient and stand firm, because the Lord's coming is near."*

_____

_____

_____

_____

Psalm 37:7a *"Be still before the Lord and wait patiently for him..."*

_____

_____

Romans 8:25 *"But if we hope for what we do not yet have, we wait for it patiently."*

Isaiah 40:31 *"Even youths grow tired and weary, and young men stumble and fall; but those who hope in the Lord will renew their strength. They will soar on wings like eagles; they will run and not grow weary, they will walk and not be faint."*

Revelation 13:10b *"...This calls for patience endurance and faithfulness on the part of the saints."*

Psalm 37:34 *"Wait for the LORD and keep his way. He will exalt you to inherit the land..."*

Your Journey

The hardest lesson requires us to be to be still and to wait patiently while we wait for God's perfect timing. We continue to receive his instruction. We are being discipled and mentored. We know that for us to be a leader in Christ, we must first learn to be an obedient follower and a servant to others.

What has caused you to want to get to the destination sooner? Why did you pick up the paddles again when you knew that you did not have the Lord's permission? Are you contemplating aborting your journey and jumping out of the canoe now? For example:

- You are in a formal training program, considering the lack of consequences if you do not complete.
- You are trying to fasttrack your education or your gaining of knowledge and understanding.
- You deem knowledge to be unimportant. On the scene "street smarts" will get you through.
- You are too stubborn or proud to listen to the counsel of your elders.
- You move away from home, despite your parents' advice to the contrary.
- You move to another city even though you have no confirmed employment.
- You sign up for a short-term mission trip and forego the formal training requirements.
- You quit your job in order to live on faith, but without God's permission.

Please accept that you have more to learn and that more refinement is required. The Lord will give you strength.

Jesus will lift you back into the canoe and you will gladly give him back the paddles. With a newfound confidence, you let the journey continue.

For Group Discussion

Share a time when you know that the Lord asked you to wait. What was the result?

Honour:
Submitting to a New Captain

How does paddling a canoe have anything to do with honour? Well, let's think about what honour means: "a good name or public esteem, reputation; of superior status, one whose worth brings respect or fame, reverence, which implies profound respect mingled with love, devotion or awe." Remember, Jesus is in the canoe. Of all the people to whom we should be showing honour, he is our first example. We may find it easy to show reverence to him, to show him respect, love and devotion. If this is really the case, then how should we honour him while we are in the canoe?

We also need to learn to move to the next stage of honour. What if the Lord brought another guide or another form of leadership into the canoe? Would you be able to honour their leadership? Would you honour the authority that their position warranted? This leadership may come in the form of our husbands, when we are told to submit to their authority. When we have been allowed to paddle the canoe ourselves or enjoy the Lord's hands on the oars, it may be very hard for us to surrender control and to trust another's hand. To honour this new hand and heart and head is a totally new experience for us.

This new captain may also be a worldly leader, such as your pastor or your workplace supervisor. No matter what their leadership style is, we are told to honour them in all that we do so that they will find it easy to lead. They will need to give account as to how they lead. For us to make their leading difficult would be unwise.

Sometimes, the captain of our canoe may be someone younger and less experienced then ourselves. Possibly, the one we are to honour is our child. No matter what they have done, or the path that they may have chosen, it is their path and not ours. As our children mature into adulthood, we need to honour their decisions and choices, just as we expect them to honour ours.

My Story

I used to think that it was very easy to honour the Lord. To honour him means to love him. To love him means to obey his commandments. Yet, how many times have I failed to obey his commandments? If I honour the Lord, I must first fear him. If I honour the Lord, then I must honour all that he has created. Do I honour my parents? Do I honour my leaders? Do I honour my husband? My children? My co-workers? Friends and neighbours? Was there a time in my life that I did not give honour where honour was due?

Sadly, I must confess that there have been many times where I have been unwilling to honour those that have been called to lead me. When my will, my sense of right and wrong, my sense of what was fair, righteous and pure got in the way, I found it very difficult to honour my leaders. That domineering and controlling boss who was given to rage was difficult for me to honour. The only way I could overcome my insubordinate spirit was to begin to pray for him. Then there was the godly leader who practiced business without integrity, and whom I perceived was unethical in his interpretation of government laws and adherence thereof. My critical spirit rose up within me and I became very judgemental. It was not until I was away from that environment that I resumed my prayers for God's guidance in his life.

Another workplace leader was probably one of the more difficult to honour because he always avoided the truth. I never knew what was expected. I never received a performance evaluation. I seldom received documented directives. I have learned that when you are dealing with an elusive leader, it is difficult to determine where the truth lies. Without truth, then how do you know which path you are to choose? On a few occasions I countered his decisions and refused to obey his directives. When I finally realized that I was the one learning the "Honour lesson", I resolved myself to the fact that he was not going to change and that I needed to move on. He was probably a very happy man when he received my resignation. The one thing that was different with this scenario is that I prayed for him constantly throughout his entire tenure as my boss. He may not have operated in truth, but I tried.

What about honouring my husband? Being a self-sufficient successful career woman meant that I did not need a provider in my life. Being led by a sexually abusive father through my child hood meant that I did not desire that sexually male influence in my life again. Having my first marriage end in divorce and spending seven years as a single mother proved that I could do all things— even move to a foreign country—without requiring a male's leadership. Therefore, one can quickly understand that submitting to my husband has been, by far, the most difficult part of my journey. In order to honour him, I must respect who he is. This I do. My husband is a man of integrity. He is faithful and consistent. He represented our country well, serving in the Canadian Forces for 21 years. He is dependable and reliable and has a sensitive heart for God. One would think it would be easy to honour this wonderful man that God had brought into my life.

Well, my husband is one of those very contented types of people. You know, the ones who are happy with a good job, going to work everyday, earning a reasonable wage, having a comfortable home and opportunities for vacations every year. As you may have gathered already, I am the exact opposite. I can seldom remember a time that I have been content. I am always looking to see what is over the next crest of the hill. There is always another mountain to climb. There is always another adventure to pursue—just because. I love being OUT of the box to see what God is going to do and my husband likes to stay IN the box. How did I learn to submit within these differences? On my knees! Either God had to change me or God had to change him and the only way that was going to happen was through prayer. I would like to say that we have met half way. Not yet, but by faith I believe that it will happen, especially as I allow God to change me. If I remain in an attitude of prayer, I will be able to honour him and submission to his guidance will be easy. Why will it be easy? Because God will have revealed his truth and his will for our lives to me through prayer.

Study Verses for Reflection:

Reflect upon these Bible verses. How do they relate to your own life? When you read them, do they offer you hope and encouragement?

Exodus 20:12a *"Honour your father and your mother..."*

_____

_____

_____

_____

1 Samuel 2:30 *"...Those who honor me I will honor..."*

_____

_____

_____

_____

Psalm 45:11b *"...honor him, for he is your lord."*

_____

_____

_____

_____

Proverbs 3:35a *"The wise inherit honour..."*

_____

_____

_____

_____

Romans12:10b *"Honor one another above yourselves."*

_____

_____

_____

_____

1 Corinthians 6:20b *"...Therefore, honour God with your body."*

_____

_____

_____

_____

Proverbs 13:18b *"...but whoever heeds corrections is honoured."*

_____

_____

_____

_____

Hebrews 13:4a *"Marriage should be honoured by all..."*

_____

_____

_____

_____

Your Journey

Surrendering the paddles to a new Captain is a challenging and stretching task. If you are accustomed to embracing independence and do not fully understand submission, then you will either refuse to let them paddle or at the very least, you will allow them only on one side of the canoe with one paddle while you control the paddling on the opposite side. I wonder how straight your course will be!

In some respects, this may be the most difficult part of our canoe journey. To truly honour those around us, we must throw out judgement and criticism. We must die to ourselves. Think for a moment about where you are at right now. Are you honouring God with your tithe? Are you submitting to your governing authorities and honouring them by paying your taxes, all of them? Are you honouring your boss? Do you honour your parents? Do you submit to your husband's leadership?

For the next few days, mediate on each of these aspects and make a point of performing some act of kindness or obedience that illustrates that you honour those around you:

- God
- Government
- Workplace
- Marriage
- Family
- Friends

When you make a habit of honouring those around you, it is amazing what God can do in your life. Being supportive and offering words of encouragement are excellent ways of giving honour.

For Group Discussion

When you honoured a member of your family or a co-worker, what happened?

Love:
Staying in the Canoe
When You Are Afraid

Perfect love casts out all fear. At least that is what the Scriptures tell us. However, have there ever been times in your life when Love was not even on your mind? A time when you were so overcome with fear that you could think of nothing else but mere survival? At what points along your canoe journey were you overcome by fear?

Let me paint another picture. You have enjoyed some very calm waters for quite some time. Almost too calm, you think! There has been no wind. The water does not even show one ripple and you feel no breeze upon your head. If anything, the air is stifling, muggy, and humid. There must be a storm approaching. You can just sense it.

What happens when the winds blow harder? What happens when the canoe begins to toss to and fro? Do you bunker down inside the canoe, lying down on your tummy and holding onto the seat clasps with all your might? Have you taken the canvas tarp and covered yourself so that you do not get wet and cold? Do you feel safe and protected?

Despite doing all these things, you probably do not feel safe. You are afraid. You are afraid that the rains will not stop. The winds will never cease. You are getting cold, wet and now very hungry. Will this night ever end? "Why is it that these storms always happen in the darkness of night anyway?!" you think. You could cope with it during the daytime because you could see what was going on. But in the night, you cannot see anything. All you can do is feel everything, and it is exactly these feelings that get you into a panic because you start to imagine the worst.

Will the canoe hit a rock and break you apart? Will all this tossing back and forth cause the seams to separate and allow the canoe to leak so you will sink? Maybe the wind is taking you totally off course and you have spent days, weeks, even months getting this far? Will you be lost? Will you be marooned on a desert island?

But wait a minute! You finally realize that you are not alone in the canoe during this terrible tempest. Jesus is in the canoe—at least he was before you started to hide under the seats. Why is he not doing something? He should be comforting you, holding you and telling you that everything is going to be okay. Where is he anyway? You slowly get up enough courage to peer out from under the canvas tarp and to your dismay, what do you discover? Yes, Jesus is still in the canoe. But is he trying to keep the canoe upright? Is he holding onto the sides for fear of falling out? Is he making intercessions to the Father to stop the storm so that the two of you can continue your peaceful journey? No. To your absolute astonishment, Jesus is asleep in the bow of the boat. He appears to not have a care in the world. "This cannot be so!" you think. Is he unconscious? Dead? "Of course not!" you remember. Jesus is alive. Then what is happening? You do not understand. In your fear, you cry out to Him.

Does Jesus answer your call? Of course, he does! His word says that when we call, he will answer. He will make a way where there is no way. His voice can calm the stormiest situation.

My Story

When I reflect upon my journey, I can recall many times when I have been afraid. During most of those times, I knew that Jesus was with me and that he and his guardian angels were protecting me.

I think of my car accident. When I realized that the car approaching me was going to make a left hand turn right in front of me and that I would certainly broadside it, I cried out "Jesus!" and he answered me. Yes, there was an accident and both cars were severely damaged. However, no one was hurt and no innocent bystanders were affected. After the impact, my car seemed to gently glide into another lane of traffic that held no moving vehicles. In addition, a witness immediately poked her head into my window and said that she had seen the entire event and confirmed that it was not my fault. The police even responded to the scene within minutes. So you see, in this case, as soon as I sensed fear, I called out to my Lord and He answered me. His perfect love cast out all fear and I knew that everything was going to be okay.

There was another time that a storm approached and fear tried to get a foothold upon my life. I was travelling alone in Europe, completing a train ride on the Orient Express between Salzburg Austria and Stuttgart, Germany. Unfortunately, I arrived at the Stuttgart train station much too late in the evening. Nonetheless, I made my way to a city train in order to complete my journey, expecting to arrive at a friend's home about thirty minutes later. When I got off the train at my supposed stop, I quickly discovered that this was the wrong station. I was in the middle of a field. The full parking lot soon became empty as other train passengers drove their cars away. I quickly found a telephone booth to call my friend and tell her that I had either taken the wrong train or disembarked at the wrong stop. Hopefully, I could pronounce where I was, or at the very least spell the Station name for her.

As I was leaning inside the phone booth, with a well-loaded backpack keeping me propped up along the side, I looked out and discovered a young man grinning at me. There was not another soul around and there he was, peering into the phone booth. "Odd way to indicate that you are waiting to make a call!" I thought. "Oh no! He does not want to make a call," I quickly realized. He had moved in front of the open phone booth door to display why he was grinning. There he was, totally exposed, playing with himself.

Now what do you think I did? Did I scream? No. As a matter of fact I firmly and rather loudly said, "In the name of Jesus, get out of here." Within seconds, or at least it seemed that way, he vanished. Obviously, my friend on the other end of the telephone had heard the entire, although limited conversation. After I explained to her what had just happened, she urged me to get out of there quickly, and I could not have agreed with her more. So, we decided where I would meet her and I called a cab to come and pick me up to drive me to our new meeting place. However, the story does not end here. When I called the cab company and they discovered where I was (I guess they could tell my location by the number of the phone booth that I gave them), they indicated that it would take about twenty minutes for someone to arrive to pick me up. "Twenty minutes!" I exclaimed and then said to myself, "I may be dead by then and they will find me raped and dragged of into the bushes. There is no way that is going to happen because me and Jesus make a majority and I am totally safe." At least, I kept telling myself that.

So, do you know what I did for the next twenty minutes? I kept the phone receiver to my ear and prayed out loud, in English, in my limited German and definitely in tongues. I prayed for absolutely everything and everyone that I could think of. That fellow would think that I was talking to a person who would immediately come to my defence. Little did he know that I was not only talking to my God, but also holding onto him and being literally surrounded by him during the entire time? Was I at peace? Through prayer, I was certainly trying. (By the way, the cab did pick me up and take me to meet my friend and the rest of my travels went without incident.)

Now, how about a time when I did give into fear? No, I can't seem to think of any. Driving on icy roads, with white knuckles gripping the steering wheel, I was confidently praying to Jesus for protection and a safe arrival at my destination. Lost in a foreign country while driving in the dark? – no. Waiting for results of medical exams? – no. Downhill skiing on black diamond runs? – no (well, maybe a little bit because I knew that I really should not have been there). As a single mother, with a young son in tow moving to Europe to take advantage of an excellent career opportunity, was I fearful? No, I knew that the Lord was directing my path. I was holding onto the promises that He had given me. On mission trips to Southeast Africa, even travelling alone, I was not afraid because I knew that Jesus was with me, protecting me and keeping me free from all manner of harm and evil. I guess I have yet to experience a kind of fear that would have me gripped with cowardice. Granted, I have not been held at knifepoint, experienced a hurricane or tornado, or been tortured in a jail cell. I would like to think that even in those incidents my faith would prevail and that I would not be afraid because my perfect love for Jesus and his perfect love for me would cast out all fear.

Study Verses for Reflection:

Reflect upon these Bible verses. How do they relate to your own life? When you read them, do they offer you hope and encouragement?

Deuteronomy 10:12 *"...what does God ask of you but to fear the Lord your God, to walk in all his ways, [and] to love him..."*

_____

_____

_____

_____

Psalm 33:18 *"But the eyes of the Lord are on those who fear him, on those who hope is in his unfailing love..."*

_____

_____

Psalm 103:11 *"So great is his love for those who fear him..."*

Psalm 118:4 *"Let those who fear the Lord say: 'His love endures forever.'"*

I John 4:18 *"There is no fear in love. But perfect love drives out fear, because fear has to do with punishment. The one who fears in not made perfect in love."*

Your Journey

Think about your current situation. Are you experiencing the darkest of nights in a wind tossed sea? Is your canoe starting to leak? Are you cold and weary and wrapped in a wet blanket too afraid to peer out from under the seat? Are you succumbing to fear? Are you thinking that Jesus is not there? Remember the poem "Footprints in the Sand." No matter what the storm is, he is always there. There are times that He even carries us through. Do not be afraid of the dark. Do not be afraid of being alone. Do not be afraid of being poor or without food. Do not be afraid of the storms of life that come your way. Remember, it is through these storms that our faith is tried and our love for our Lord Jesus is tested and proven to be solid.

The next time you consider entering into an emotional state of fear, call upon the name of the Lord Jesus and you will be surprised at what happens. The storms may continue, but you will have a peace and an assurance that everything is going to be okay. Your perfect love for Him will cast out all manner of fear.

Remember a quote from my husband: "When fear comes knocking at your door, answer it with faith, and when you open the door, nothing will be there."

For Group Discussion

Ministering angels of protection are always around us. When have you been aware of the impact of their presence?

Joy: Throwing Everything Out of the Canoe

"Consider it pure joy whenever you face trials of many kinds."

(James 1:2)

Even if there are no storms, there may be other times in your journey when you may want to lie down and cover up your head. This is when there is no joy in the journey. It has taken too long. The sun is too hot, or maybe it is too cold. It has been too difficult. You do not like the person that has been chosen to captain the vessel. You do not like the shore that you've been washed up on, so you simply lay down and hope to die.

Can you relate to this? Have there been times when you did not want to play anymore? Give up? Check out? Fall asleep and hope that you do not wake up? The darker the blanket the better!

These times usually occur when we are facing trials. But instead of counting these trials as "pure joy" we perceive them to be a form of penance. We figure we must have done something wrong and God is punishing us. Much like our earthly fathers may have done, we are being disciplined. We begin to relate to the book of Job. Our health has been attacked. Deaths of loved ones around us have impacted us greatly. We have lost all our possessions and our friends have abandoned us. Even those who still hang around us are not very encouraging. Even the ones closest to us are telling us to "curse God and die." Are you able to think as Job did at the beginning of his suffering? This is illustrated in Job 2:10 which states, "Shall we not accept good from God, and not trouble?"

Or are you more able to identify with the Job of chapter 3, which starts with, "May the day of my birth perish..." and continues through the entire chapter with how he wishes he had never been born. You are constantly chanting to yourself, "Nobody likes me, everybody hates me... if I disappeared or died tomorrow, nobody would miss me." You may have gone past mere depression to the point of considering suicide.

My Story

A reality that has been difficult for me to accept is the perceived absence of joy in my life. Why? I have struggled with seasons of depression for so long that they seem normal and the thought of experiencing longer seasons of joy escapes me. If I wasn't already saved, I would tell myself to give my life to Christ and he would make my joy complete. Well, I have learned that, for me anyway, it is not instant. Much like with other forms of diseases, (by the way, I finally accepted that depression is a mental illness) sometimes God miraculously heals and sometimes he does not. It may be a "thorn in our side" much like what Paul experienced, or the Lord may wish us to journey through the healing process with him so that our victory can be more complete. I have decided to press on, one day at a time. Each day starts out with my requested and accepted assistance from Jesus.

Before I became a Christian, I journeyed from psychiatrists, to therapists, to counsellors, and back again, trying to seek treatment for my depressive condition. One prescribed medication, while another said that hypnosis and other forms of meditative techniques would heal me. Then another said that a series of counselling sessions would see me set free. Naturally, none of them worked. Medication would only hide the symptoms. Secular therapy would only bring the causes to the surface, with only my own mental forbearance to work through the web. There was no assistance from the ultimate Healer of all—Jesus Christ.

Then I became a Christian. Did the depression go away? Yes, for a time it did because I was caught up in those new believer emotions. However, we all know that these feelings soon subside and the realities of day-to-day living begin to greet us with force. God allowed me to coast along for about eighteen months before the "honeymoon" phase was over. My jolt back to reality came with a nervous breakdown. Yes, a Christian can experience a mental collapse. With the aid of my pastor, a Christian physician and a Christian counsellor, I accepted that the Lord had allowed this to happen so that he could begin to heal those deeply rooted causes of the emotional side of my illness. That is when I realized that this was going to be a process. After about six months of therapy, I was able to resume my career, knowing that, with the Lord's help, I could overcome those seasons of despair by relying on the strength of the Lord. I could do all things through Christ who strengthens me—a verse I would quote on a regular basis. I would be transformed by the renewing of my mind by listening to Christian music and reading the Bible. With my requested help from the Lord, each day could be a victory.

Now that I have been a Christian for almost twenty years, I must confess that this has not always been easy. There were many times when I chose not to ask for help and instead wallowed in my despair. I wanted to have a pity party and some of those parties lasted much longer than they needed to. Those loved ones closest around me often got drawn down into the muck as well.

One of those significant times occurred shortly after I returned to Canada from Germany, married and eight months pregnant. The excitement of moving into a new city, building a brand new house and giving birth to a beautiful little boy soon disappeared. The reality of this new life soon came crashing down, and I mean crashing. Not only was I going to experience postpartum blues, but also the effects of reverse culture shock would soon become quite obvious. I missed those quaint little German coffee shops, the markets, the scenery, the driving, and the simple efficiency in which they lived their lives. I began to despise everything Canadian—the waste, the inefficient use of our beautiful land, the poor drivers, and the lack of a "market" shopping experience. I was faced with super malls, wide streets, rutted freeways, inconsiderate drivers, and noise, noise, noise. There was no such thing as quiet on Sundays. Everybody seemed to be working. Everything was open for business and the construction workers were busy operating their heavy equipment early in the morning—a morning that should be a "day of rest". Oh, how I wanted to go back to Europe! Now, combine that with the emotional effects of giving birth and you have a prime setting for depression to set in.

Despite having gone through this routine previously, I still found myself staring at this little bundle and wondering how I was ever going to cope with caring for him. My career was not merely on hold—I was convinced that it was done. I was certain that I no longer had the mental forbearance to continue on in the opportunities and challenges that I welcomed in the past. Yes, I admit, this was not an easy time. However, with the help of a loving husband, a wonderful church family and some great neighbours, a calming routine began to take shape and it was not long before I knew that I could cope. As a matter of fact, just like clockwork, when my six-month maternity leave was over I was ready to go back to work.

There was another time, a time that was not that long ago, when depression came to visit in a significant way yet once again. I was well aware that by keeping my life full and busy the desperate sinking feeling would not haunt me. Yet, I knew that I needed a rest. It was becoming quite apparent that I could no longer continue with the career pace which I found myself in. My health was suffering, my family was suffering and my spiritual walk was faltering. With a great step of courage, I resigned from my job and took a sabbatical. Since I initially planned this time of respite to be only six months, I was confident that with a good home routine and a daily discipline that included physical exercise, prayer, reading my Bible and volunteering, those little demons of depression would not get in. Well, the sabbatical lasted a full year and it wasn't long before those ghosts that were over my shoulder moved right in front of my face and I sank.

Boy, did I sink! There were days that I got up, took my son to school and then came right back home to bed. When I awoke for the second time, I would open another box of chocolates and inhale them. At least, I must have inhaled them, because they disappeared so fast that there is no way I could have eaten them. But eat them I did. In one week alone, I consumed three Pot of Gold boxes of chocolates. How did I get out if it? How did I rise above the miry clay? By admitting, yet once again, that I had a problem and that I needed help. Okay doctor; prescribe the medication. This time in a stronger dosage so that it will work! I promise that I will take it.

The choice is mine to make. Each day I must remember to take up my cross (in this case my mental illness) and walk as Jesus would have walked.

Once I accepted the fact that this form of illness is no different than having diabetes, poor eyesight or hearing difficulty, I realized that, if necessary, medical assistance must be okay. A Christian diabetic still takes insulin, even though they continue to pray for God to miraculously heal them. A Christian with a hearing problem will continue to wear the hearing aid while waiting for their miracle. If the Christian has poor eyesight, whether developed early in life or as a result of old age, he will put on his glasses to help him see better. If the doctor prescribes anti-depressants to treat my condition, then why not accept his assistance? Someday I hope to have that miracle in my life, but if God so chooses for me to have this infirmity until the day I die, I know that he will give me the strength to carry through. All I have to do is ask for it.

There may be times when I may think that I am walking through the valley of the shadow of death. Nevertheless, there will be another mountaintop. Since I crave the mountaintops, each one higher than the other, than I need to be prepared to face the valleys of the shadows of death before each difficult journey—a journey that always results in another glorious discovery.

Study Verses for Reflection:

Reflect upon these Bible verses. How do they relate to your own life? When you read them, do they offer you hope and encouragement?

Deuteronomy 16:15b *"...and your joy will be complete."*

_____

_____

_____

_____

Nehemiah 8:10 *"...for the joy of the Lord is your strength."*

_____

_____

_____

_____

Psalm 45:7b *"...by anointing you with the oil of joy."*

_____

_____

_____

_____

Hebrews 12:2 *"...for the joy set before him, he endured..."*

_____

_____

_____

_____

James 1:2 *"Consider it pure joy, my brothers, when you face trials..."*

_____

_____

_____

_____

2 Timothy 1:4b *"...so that I may be filled with joy."*

_____

_____

_____

_____

2 Corinthians 12:7, 9a *"To keep me from becoming conceited because of these surpassingly great revelations, there was given me a thorn in my flesh, a messenger of Satan, to torment me. ...But the Lord said to me, 'My grace is sufficient for you, my power is made perfect in weakness'."* (This is one of my favourite passages.)

_____

_____

_____

_____

_____

Your Journey

What are you struggling with? Are you also fighting depression? Statistics indicate that clinical depression can affect people of all ages, either sex, and all socio-economic and ethnic backgrounds. "Depression is the most common serious psychiatric illness. Some 10 to 15 percent of people suffer from it at some time in their lives, especially in the milder forms."* There doesn't seem to be any one clear cause for clinical depression. Instead, a number of different factors have been found to play a role in the development of clinical depression:

- A particular trauma (e.g. the death of a loved one, the loss of a job, the break-up of a significant relationship, the diagnosis of a major illness).
- Periods of prolonged stress.
- A physical or viral illness.
- Some hormonal imbalances (such as a low level of thyroid hormone or the hormonal changes that occur following childbirth).
- A familial tendency towards the development of depression—in these cases it isn't always clear whether it's a person's genes or something in a person's upbringing that contributes to the tendency to develop depression in certain families.
- Sensitivity to a reduction in the amount of sunlight that one is exposed to.
- The development of a clinical depression can be a consequence of using some street drugs as well as prescription medications.
- Newer research indicates that imbalances of certain chemicals in the brain, called neurotransmitters, play a role in clinical depression. What is not clear, however, is how the levels of neurotransmitters lose their balance and whether the imbalance contributes to the development of the depression OR occurs as a result of the depression. Newer forms of

antidepressant medications do work, however, by restoring the balance of neurotransmitters in the brain.

- In some cases, no contributing factors appear obvious in the development of a bout of depression.

* Reference: The Canadian Medical Association - Home Medical Encyclopaedia, Dr Peter Morgan (Editor), The Reader's Digest Association (Canada) Ltd., Montreal, 1992.

If you are having a difficult time trying to experience the joy that can be overflowing, then your challenge may be more than temporary. Seek Christian counselling. Allow a doctor to effectively diagnose you and, if necessary, prescribe an anti-depressant. Finally, on a daily basis, claim some of the Scriptures that I previously referenced.

Remember, you are not alone. You are not a second-class believer. When you read through your Bible, you will quickly discover that you are not alone. Some of our biblical patriarchs also suffered from depression or despondency. Moses said in Numbers 11:15, "If this is how you are going to treat me, put me to death right now..." Elijah said in 1 Kings 19:4, after he had gone a day's journey into the dessert, "I have had enough, Lord. Take my life; I am no better than my ancestors." As well, when we revisit my previous reference to Job, further illustrated in Job 10:1 when he said, "I loathe my very life; therefore I will give free rein to my complaint and speak out in the bitterness of my soul." Even David had his moments, as illustrated in Psalm 42:6 when he said, "My soul is downcast within me..." When you read through the gospels, you discover that the disciples had moments of feeling downcast or depressed.

Knowing that we are not alone certainly has given me encouragement. If my Bible heroes persevered through their moments of despondency and affliction, then I can be encouraged to do the same.

For Group Discussion

Share your current situation. Are you "on top of the world" or are you wondering how you are going to make it through another day?

Hope:
Stranded with No Wind

This chapter is actually a last minute add-in, for I thought this book was finished. Then a hesitation came with the realization that there was one more chapter to write. As I was pondering about what this chapter would be about, I understood that it would involve something that I was yet to walk through. Even as I write, I am experiencing this part of my journey. A phase where all one has is Hope.

When you continue on your canoe journey, what is the best illustration of hope? At what point in the journey do we have absolutely nothing but HOPE? We can do nothing. No crying, no screaming, and no manipulating can manoeuvre our way out of the circumstances. We cannot orchestrate anything. No matter what we do, doors remain closed and windows are shut. We may even feel as though we have been "grounded" by our heavenly Father. You begin to think that you may have done something wrong, and the Lord is disciplining you. Possibly, he wishes to remind you to honour some long ago promise. Simply being still is not even on your mind, as you analyze all the reasons why the wind is not blowing.

Now imagine this. You are all alone in the canoe. The Lord has physically left you on your own. "I trust you!" He says before he departs.

"Wow," you think, "God actually trusts me. After all the difficulties that I have been through, all my stubbornness and all the discipline that He has had to enforce, He actually trusts me." However, before he left you on your own, he says to you "Now, this next lesson will be about you trusting me."

"Not a problem," you think, "I am a skilled oarsman now. I am a mature Christian. I can do this." Then the Lord says that he is taking the paddles with him as you will no longer require them. Instead, he has equipped your boat with a sail. You are quite excited because with the wind in your sail, you will move through this journey much faster. You begin to anticipate the wind, that gentle breeze that cools you on a hot summer day. The one that refreshes you during an autumn walk in the woods. The fresh breeze that comes after a spring rain. (You have deliberately ignored the fierce north wind that may come in the winter.) "This will be great," you say to yourself.

But then, the wind dies down. It is non-existent. You are in the middle of a large body of water and you cannot see land on any of the horizons. You are "dead in the water." You remember that you cannot paddle anywhere, because the paddles are gone. You cannot start up an engine, because this boat did not come equipped with one. All you have is a sail, which is of little good when there is no wind. No ingenuity can craft anything that could remotely resemble a paddle. Minimal provisions and the reality of a hot sun are the only known facts.

In our Christian walk, we often yearn for times like these, because it forces us to slow down. We relax, take a retreat, and enjoy some quiet time. However, what happens when this quiet time drags on; when there is no action, no wave, and no wind? Do we become anxious? Do we fear what may be in the water? Do we fear that we will we not have enough provision and that we will die from hunger or thirst? Will Jesus really come back for us? Will he command the wind to blow? How long will we be like this?

You remember the promises that God has given you. You know the plans that He has for you. However, right now, all you can do is fight off discouragement and hold on to hope.

My Story

As a write this, I am stranded in the middle of the ocean. My paddles have been replaced with a sail but there is no wind. My provisions are to the point of rations. There is barely enough for tomorrow. My lips are blistered from the relentless beating of the hot summer sun, and my throat is parched from lack of water. "I am so thirsty!" I cry out, as I look at the salty water around me. My body is weak and listless as there has been no food to eat. What got me to this point?

About eighteen months ago, I felt the Lord's urging to leave my place of employment and enjoy a time of rest and rejuvenation. At the beginning of this sabbatical, I was able to follow my life-long dream of writing. In addition, I was called upon to conduct corporate training seminars across Canada. Following my deep passion for the peoples of Africa, I volunteered my time and talent to a new African medical relief association. After about a year, (which was longer than I had anticipated), I began to feel refreshed and refocused, thinking that I had completed my sabbatical, whereby I had the opportunity to enhance my international business consulting skills and develop my corporate training and facilitation abilities. These new experiences, combined with over twenty years in the corporate world would surely warrant being a sought after executive.

During the subsequent few months I began to contact several executive search agencies that consistently informed me that the market was "hot" and that I should have no problem enhancing my life with an additional employment contract. In addition, lunching with friends and colleagues and responding to numerous "help wanted" ads gave me hope that it would not be long before I was "back in the saddle." In the meantime, I was keeping actively engaged with continued corporate training requests complimented with a part-time consulting contract. I had nothing to fear. Suddenly, the workshops ceased. No matter what I did, whom I called, or whom I met with, no one could advise why I was no longer on the active speaker list. Four months passed with my only contribution to the family coffers being a minimal honorarium. Considering what I was earning before, this brought a significant change to our family's lifestyle. This, in itself, was difficult to grasp, but added to this was our prior decision to build another home.

Considering I was already on contractual work, why were we building a home? Because God told us to! Without going into the entire story, both my husband and I believed that what we were doing was right and under God's full blessing. Our current home had almost doubled in value, indicating that this was the time to sell so we could use the equity to build again in another new neighbourhood. At the beginning, everything was going smoothly. Three different realtors plus the bank's appraisal confirmed that the city's assessed value of our property was correct. Knowing what we could sell our home for and knowing what we could build in the new area at a reasonable price, we realized that our household debt would decrease. My husband and I were so excited because that meant we would finally be in the place of being able to give more to those ministries who were in need of support. We had even agreed on which of the "poor, widow, and orphan" programs located in "Jerusalem, Judea, and the outer most parts of the earth" that we would begin to support.

Well guess what? It has been almost seven months and our home still has not sold. We had two offers, both of which have fallen through. And you guessed it! The investment in our new home is coming in a little bit higher than we had planned. We are quickly realizing that we will be fortunate if we break even.

One afternoon, while I was meditating on this fact, the Lord was quick to reveal to me that it is not about the finances, nor our desire to decrease our debt, nor our desire to give more "offerings." He knows our hearts and He said that he trusts us. This is about something altogether different. He is doing a new thing in my husband and I. He wants to bring us to a new place in him. This whole experience is about us trusting him. "Okay, Lord," I prayed, "I trust you. You are the great 'I AM.' With your words the earth was formed in six days. You speak and the winds cease. You are omnipotent. You are our provider. You know all things and see all things. You are in control."

Realization is quickly settling in that I am no longer in control of anything. God has full control—so much so that he has taken away my paddles (my ability to work and contribute financially to our family) and the wind out of my sails (my ability to move). No matter what I try, the phone calls, the meetings, the letters, no additional prospective employment is on the horizon. No matter what we do with our realtors, what we do to "stage" our home, people still continually go through our home, say it is beautiful, but walk away just the same. We are marketing our home to tickle all their dreams and emotions and still they walk away. At one point, we even attempted renting our home. Owning two properties was going to be a bit risky, but if that was what we had to do to get ourselves out of this bind, we were willing to do so.

As I write this chapter, I can give no ending—only a promise. Romans 12:12 says that we are to "Be joyful in hope, patient in affliction, faithful in prayer." Faithful in prayer seems to be the easy part right now. Because we are so desperate, we are constantly on our knees calling out to God for our daily bread and the release from these circumstances. Yet, I see what God has done in uniting our family through these consistent daily devotional times. God is doing an enormous work in my husband. His faith is solid and he has truly taken over the priesthood of our home. (Hmm...I guess that is an answer to all those pleading prayers with the Lord over the years). The patient in affliction part has not been easy but still we preserve. It is somewhat humbling when every conversation leads to someone asking if your home has sold yet, and you have to reply "No." At one point we began to believe that there really must be something wrong with our home if no one wants to live in it. However, through it all, we have been constantly reminded that God is in control. His timing is perfect and He has a greater purpose being fulfilled through this season of waiting. Since He said that He trusts us, then He must know that we can be patient through these circumstances.

We have begun to realize that this season is probably having a greater spiritual impact on all those around us. Since we only see the situational circumstances, it has been difficult to embrace the fact that God is using our willingness to be patient to affect a great many others. That brings us to Hope. Are we joyful in hope? If I focus on the promises of God, yes there is joy. But when I focus on the circumstances, well, that is another matter all together.

Study Verses for Reflection:

Reflect upon these Bible verses. How do they relate to your own life? When you read them, do they offer you hope and encouragement?

Romans 12:12 *"Be joyful in hope, patient in affliction, faithful in prayer."*

_____
_____
_____
_____

Job 13:15a *"Though he slay me, yet will I hope in him..."*

_____
_____
_____
_____

Isaiah 40:31 *"...but those who hope in the Lord will renew their strength. They will soar on wings like eagles; they will run and not grow weary, they will walk and not be faint."*

_____

_____

_____

_____

Jeremiah 29:11 *" 'For I know the plans that I have for you,' declares the Lord, 'plans to prosper you and not to harm you, plans to give you hope and a future.' "*

_____

_____

_____

_____

Hebrews 11:1 *"Now faith is being sure of what we hope for and certain of what we do not see."*

_____

_____

_____

_____

Your Journey

Are you at a place in your life where you thought that you were "all grown up in Christ?" A place where you have graduated from paddles to a sail, only to discover that with paddles you were sometimes in control, but with sails, you are at the mercy of the wind? Now that you are stranded in the middle of the ocean, what are you doing? Are you whining and complaining? Have you given up? Have you buried the promises of God?

Meditate for a moment on another Scripture, I Corinthians 13:13, which states that, "Now these three remain: faith, hope and love..." How can you know what hope is if you have not been taught? How can you receive the blessing that comes to those whose Hope is in the Lord if you do not walk (or should I say wait) through these desperate and trying times in your life?

Without allowing God to weave the quality of Hope in your life, you will not be able to mount up like an eagle. You will not be in that place of allowing God to prosper you and give you a future. Hope comes first; the rewards come later. It is not the other way around. As difficult as it may seem, these are the times in your life when you need to embrace His word. You need to be around other brothers and sisters in the faith who can encourage you. You may feel like you are being tested like Job, but hold onto the end of the story. What Job had at the end was greater than what he had in the beginning. Receive this season of your life as a gift because it means that God is bringing you into something great.

For Group Discussion

In your Christian journey, explain a time when you knew that you were standing on a promise of God. How long did you have to wait? What were the results?

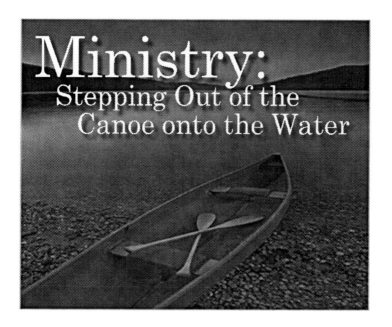

Ministry:
Stepping Out of the Canoe onto the Water

The time has come for you to complete the journey. You have reached the ocean and the Lord has stopped the canoe. Jesus asks you to step out of the boat. "But Lord, there is no shore here! The ocean is vast," you explain. "If I get out of the boat, I shall sink again. I do not have the strength to swim, Lord. Or do you actually wish for me to walk on water? How will my footing be established? I will sink. It is too dangerous!" you cry.

As a result of all this self-talk, you refuse to get out of the boat. Besides, the boat is very comfortable. You have had the chance to fix it up real nice. You have come to enjoy the special intimate relationship that only you and Jesus have had for so long. You have learned not only to honour and submit to the other leadership provided in the boat, you actually now hide behind it (i.e. your husband, your children, your religious traditions). Why do you have to get wet? Why do you have to use your own strength again? It is simply going to be too difficult.

However, Jesus reminds you that it is not your strength that will prevail. It is His strength that will be made perfect in your weaknesses. Yes, you may be comfortable and very contented, but you will never experience the true joy or satisfaction of being a disciple of Christ if you do not get out of the boat. You must get out of your comfort zone and walk where Jesus wants you to walk. Be where Jesus wants you to be. Talk with whom Jesus wants you to talk with. Encourage those whom the Lord brings around you. Love those that God places along your path. As my pastor's wife recently said, you must walk through the veil. You must have the courage to leave that which is comfortable. This is ministry.

My Story

Although there may have been many false starts, there has always been one distinct call upon my life with respect to ministry. In October 1992, at an International Women's Aglow Conference in Prague, Czechoslovakia, God said he was going to use my hands to heal women. That day I knew that I was called to Women's Ministry. Yet, until recently, which is now more than ten years later, I fought that calling. I wanted nothing to do with Women's Ministry. Although I had tried to lead Ladies' Bible studies, there had been no growth. I wanted nothing to do with Mother's groups, weekly craft gatherings or tea and fellowship. I was a businesswoman and my sphere of influence involved mostly businessmen. The businesswomen around me were either competitors or my subordinates. How on earth could I be involved with this?

Yet, here I am, watching my ministry unfold before me. I have gotten out of the boat and Jesus is teaching me to walk on water. I realized that if I did not get out of the boat when the Lord called, I would be pulled back by the undercurrent of well-meaning family and friends. I could not allow the undercurrent to take me backwards, when the journey to get this far had been so difficult and rewarding.

Go ahead river; let the undercurrent take the canoe. I am walking on water with my Jesus. I do not need the canoe's safety any longer. I am willing to step back into leadership, not hiding as the 2 I.C. (second in command), but as a submissive servant to Jesus.

What does walking on water mean to me? It means walking away from my fear of poverty. It means walking away from my need for a title or accomplishments. It means being without a job, trusting the Lord to supply my needs. As I pen this book, I am only getting sporadic contract work and my husband has recently been laid off. As a couple, God is taking us out of the boat. Our comfort zones, our boxes, are being destroyed. We have no choice but to trust in Him and follow His call. Where will this call take us? I am giddy with excitement and anticipation waiting for the adventure to unfold. I know my God and I know that no matter what happens, He will never leave me stranded and begging for bread. That means I shall never be hungry. No weapon formed against me shall prosper, so that means that He will ensure victory in all life's battles that come my way. I can confidently say, "Okay, world, here I come. I've got the glory of the Lord as my strength. I have angels encamped around me."

Study Verses for Reflection:

Reflect upon these Bible verses. How do they relate to your own life? When you read them, do they offer you hope and encouragement?

John 15:7-8 *"If you remain in me and my words remain in you, ask whatever you wish and it will be given to you. This is to my Father's glory, that you bear much fruit, showing yourself to be my disciples."*

_____

_____

_____

_____

Philippians 4:13 *"I can do all things through him who gives me strength."*

_____

_____

_____

_____

1 Peter 4:10-11a *"Each one should use whatever gift he has received...if anyone speaks, he should do it as one speaking the very word of God. If anyone serves, he should do it with the strength that God provides..."*

_____

_____

_____

_____

2 Corinthians 12:10 *"That is why, for Christ's sake, I delight in weakness, in insults, in hardships, in persecution, in difficulties. For when I am weak, then I am strong."*

_____
_____
_____
_____

James 1:27 *"Religion that God our Father accepts as pure and faultless is this: to look after orphans and widow in their distress and to keep oneself from being polluted by the world."*

_____
_____
_____
_____

Micah 6:8 *"He has showed you, O man, what is good. And what does the Lord require of you? To act justly and to love mercy and to walk humbly with your God."*

_____
_____
_____
_____

Matthew 5:44-45a *"But I tell you: Love your enemies and pray for those who persecute you that you may be sons of your Father in heaven."*

_____
_____
_____
_____

Romans 12:20 *"...If your enemy is hungry, feed him; if he is thirsty, give him something to drink. In doing this, you will heap burning coals on his head."*

_____
_____

111

_____

_____

2 Corinthians 5:18 *"All this is from God, who reconciled us to himself through Christ and gave us the ministry of reconciliation: that God was reconciling the world to himself in Christ, not counting men's sins against them. And he has committed to us the message of reconciliation."*

_____

_____

_____

_____

Psalm 32:8 *"I will instruct you and teach you in the way you should go; I will counsel you and watch over you."*

_____

_____

_____

_____

Your Journey

When it is time to step out in faith and embrace your destiny, you must remember one thing. You cannot walk on water if you do not get out of the canoe. It may only be for a brief moment in time, but you must let go of this comfortable season in your life before you can grab hold of the next promise.

Remember, Jesus will give you the strength. You will not minister in your own strength, as you tried to do in the past. When the Lord called Peter out of the boat, he obeyed. "Okay Lord," you promise, "If Peter could walk on water, then I can, too. Only help me to keep my eyes on you so that I do not lose my footing and sink."

Now—out of the boat!

For Group Discussion

Share with the group an area of ministry that you believe that the Lord has called you to. If you are not certain, then describe the skills and interests that you hold.

Conclusion:

I trust that you have enjoyed this book. Maybe you used it as your own personal devotional. Maybe you walked through it with other women as part of a Bible Study. Whatever brought you through this book; my prayer is that my journey, my struggles and my victories have been an encouragement to you. I have finally realized that I cannot be a strong believer without the fellowship of the saints, and in particular, other women. I cannot move forward unless I am vulnerable and I am not vulnerable until I remove the veil from my face. If I want to see God, then the veil must come off my eyes. Once the veil is removed, not only will I see God, but also, others can see the real me. "Blessed are the pure in heart, for they will see God." Our eyes are the windows of our soul.

Are you in the canoe? Then please sit down. If Jesus is paddling the canoe, then relax and enjoy his fellowship. If the canoe is journeying to a distant shore of unforgiveness, welcome the opportunity to be set free. Maybe you are questioning the direction of the current and want to try a different course. Are you supposed to be paddling? Then it is time to pick up a paddle and start learning how—not too fast and not too slow, but in time with Jesus. Are you not allowing Jesus to paddle? Are you trying to stay in control and steer the course yourself? Are you trying to navigate the rapids alone? What passengers have you been asked to take on? Has Jesus given you a new captain? Has He asked you to lighten your load? Maybe you are stranded without any wind. But then again, maybe that is a signal for you to get out and start walking on the water.

Be encouraged. We have all been on this journey. You will learn each step of the way. The saints that have gone on before us are encouraging us to keep going.

Be blessed.

Printed in the United States
72278LV00002B/1-99

9 781894 928618